doublestitch

DESIGNS FOR THE CROCHET FASHIONISTA

erika + monika simmons

INTERWEAVE PRESS

PHOTOGRAPHY: brian steege EXCEPT FOR
THE FOLLOWING PAGES BY brooks freehill:
3, 4 bottom left, 18–21, 30–33, 44–57, 58–63,
66–69, 78–81, 88–91, 120.
COVER AND INTERIOR DESIGN: karla baker
TECHNICAL EDITOR: donna druchunas

Text © 2008 Erika and Monika Simmons
Photography © 2008 Interweave Press LLC
Illustrations © 2008 Interweave Press LLC

Interweave Press LLC
201 East Fourth Street
Loveland, CO 80537-5655 USA
interweavebooks.com

Printed in China through Asia Pacific Offset

Library of Congress Cataloging-in-Publication
Data

Simmons, Erika, 1972-
  Double stitch : designs for the crochet fash-
ionista / Erika and Monika Simmons, authors.
     p. cm.
  Includes index.
  ISBN 978-1-59668-063-0 (pbk.)
  1. Crocheting--Patterns. 2. Dress accessories.
I. Simmons, Monika, 1972- II. Title.
  TT825.S5443 2008
  746.43'4--dc22

  2007036775

10 9 8 7 6 5 4 3 2 1

This book is dedicated to God for gracing us with this opportunity to share our gift of crochet design with the world.

Thanks to our Family: Momma, Grandma, Sekani, Toni, and Kim for inspiring us to start crocheting in the first place and for setting the stage for us to Act, Feel, and Be superstars in all of our endeavors!

Thanks to Chris and Nyree for their constant love and support throughout our growth as human beings and artists.

Special thanks to our fourth grade teacher, Mrs. Pugh, for introducing us to the art of crochet.

Thanks to our wonderful Sista-preneurs, Malaun, Vershawn, Doni, Dale, Jocelyn, Tiffany, Kelley, Akua, Erika B, etc. . . . for supporting us in our quest to keep "Doing what we love."

A super special thanks to Jada Russell for her vision and dedication to getting the Double Stitch name out there.

Thank you to Gwen Blakley Kinsler for introducing us to the world of Interweave Press in our first *Interweave Crochet* article, thus leading to this book.

Many thanks to the entire Interweave Press team for keeping us on track and teaching us the "book writing" ropes every step of the way: Tricia Waddell, Katrina Vogel, Donna Druchunas, Rebecca Campbell, Jaime Guthals, and Laura Levaas.

Thanks to Karla, Brian, Monica, and Cass for their upbeat attitudes and obvious talent that made shooting our first book a wonderful experience.

And, of course, thanks to Lori Jean for her patience and pattern-writing expertise.

INTRODUCTION

We first learned to crochet in an after-school program when we were in the fourth grade. We could not have known at the time that crochet would eventually carry us to where we are today. As models, dancers, fitness instructors, and professional hair braiders, we've spent many years observing the business of fashion, as well as health, beauty, and entertainment. These experiences, along with a renewed interest in crochet as adults, led us to launch our own crochet accessories line in 2002. The fledgling business rapidly expanded into a full fashion line that has been featured in numerous print publications and on television. Today the Double Stitch brand has a broad fan base stretching from New York to Los Angeles. This just goes to show—don't forget those arts and crafts you learned as a kid—you never know what could happen when you pull them out and get creative!

The next step in cultivating Double Stitch was to write this book for the crochet fashionista, that artistic individual who is ready to take the leap into crocheting fabulous garments and accessories that will turn heads and stop traffic. No matter what you do, or where you call home, you will find fantastic projects in the pages of this book to fit a variety of occasions and seasons.

As twin sisters, we find ourselves constantly looking for new ways to put our own personal stamp on an outfit so that our individual personalities and sense of style come through in our clothing. As women, we are committed to flattering the female body and accentuating feminine silhouettes of all shapes and sizes. You will find that many of the garments featured in this book are adjustable through lacing. Others feature an easy fit and airy, open structure without becoming shapeless or—heaven forbid—boring! Details like fringe, ruffles, and loops along with unique color combinations make these projects a perfect way to inject a little fun into your wardrobe. The construction also happens to be deceptively simple, due to our unique methods such as crocheting in the round, which often eliminates the need for seams. Whether you just want a crochet accessory to add to an outfit or you want to jump in with both feet and wear crochet from head to toe, we've covered it all! We have brought these fresh designs direct from the runway to your crochet hook, so grab some beautiful yarn and get started. And just think—the next time someone wants to know where you got such a great outfit, you can proudly say "I made it myself."

erika + monika

OUT AND ABOUT

Whether you're heading out to spend a day at the beach, at the office, or just running errands around town, you'll want to look fabulous doing it! This section is full of flattering, feminine silhouettes, and unique designs for every season. We love chic alternatives to what everyone else is wearing, such as overhead sleeves instead of a cardigan or a cozy poncho instead of a jacket. Soon you'll be wearing crochet in ways you never imagined and loving every minute of it! Get ready for fun, funky, and functional crochet that will be sure to gain you some admirers.

deep-vhalter
WITH FRINGE

Believe it or not, this halter top was designed with a little coverage in mind. The fringe adds visual length, allowing you to maintain a little more mystery than a traditional cropped top would allow while creating sexy drama. This top is the perfect choice for anything from an afternoon pool party to evening cocktails.

finished size
S (M, L) sized to fit 30–32 (34–36, 38–40)" (76.5–81.5 [86.5–91.5, 96.5–102] cm) bust circumference (exact size is determined by adjustable ties).

finished measurements
About 17¼ (19½, 22)" (44 [49.5, 56] cm) across bottom edge (exact circumference determined by ties) and 36 (36½, 37)" (91.5 [93, 94] cm) long with fringe.

yarn
Worsted weight (# 4 Medium).

WE USED: TLC Cotton Plus (51% cotton, 49% acrylic; 178 yd [163 m]/3½ oz [100 g]):1 (1, 1) ball #3643 kiwi (A); 2 (2, 3) balls #3615 jazz multi (B).

hook
Size G/6 (4 mm). Adjust hook size if necessary to obtain correct gauge.

notions
Removable markers; tapestry needle.

gauge
13 hdc and 12 rows = 4" (10 cm).

HALTER TOP

With A, ch 57 (61, 65).

ROW 1 (RS): Sc in 2nd ch from hook and in each ch across, turn—56 (60, 64) dc.

RIGHT FRONT

ROW 2 (WS): Ch 2 (counts as hdc), hdc in next 27 (29, 31) sc, turn.

Continue working on this half of the front only.

ROW 3: Ch 1, sc2tog, sc in each hdc to last 2 hdc, sc2tog, turn.

ROW 4: Ch 2 (counts as hdc), hdc in each sc to end, turn.

Rep Rows 3 and 4 until 6 sts rem. End after working a WS row.

NEXT 6 ROWS: Ch 3 (counts as dc), dc in each st across, turn.

If necessary, continue working in dc until piece measures 14½ (15, 15½)" (36 [38, 39.5] cm) or is long enough to reach around to center back neck. Fasten off. Weave in end.

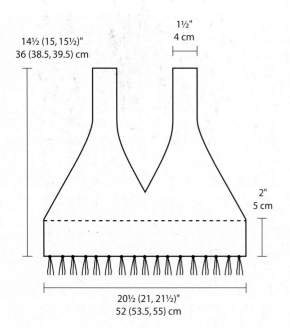

14½ (15, 15½)"
36 (38.5, 39.5) cm

1½"
4 cm

2"
5 cm

20½ (21, 21½)"
52 (53.5, 55) cm

LEFT FRONT

Join A to first unworked st of Row 1. Mark this st. Ch 2 (counts as hdc), hdc in each of next 27 sc, turn.

Beg at Row 3, rep instructions for Right Front.

Do not fasten off. Sl st last row of Left Front to last row of Right Front at back neck. Fasten off. Weave in end.

FINISHING

Turn piece around, with RS facing, join B to first st of foundation ch.

ROW 1 (RS): Sc in each ch across, turn.

ROWS 2–4: Ch 1, sc across, turn.

ROW 5: Ch 1, sc across, do not turn.

RND 6: Sc evenly around entire piece. Fasten off. Weave in end.

PICOT EDGE: With RS facing, join B to top edge of short end at back * Ch 4, sk next sc, sc in next sc; rep from * along short edge, across bottom of halter, and along opposite short edge. Fasten off. Weave in end.

FRONT TRIM: With RS facing, join B marked st of Left Front, sc evenly around front opening. Continue to sl st first and last 6 sts of rnd tog. Fasten off. Weave in end.

FRINGE: With B, cut 112 strands, each 48" (122 cm) long. Fold in half. Knot 4 strands held tog into each ch-4 lp across bottom of piece by pulling strands through the loop and pulling tight.

TIE: With B, ch 120. Fasten off. Weave through bottom three ch-4 lps on each side of back opening. Tie into a bow.

Lightly block halter top.

webbed halter

DRESS

Way too often, we find ourselves at the beach, a party, or a picnic dressed like everyone else. Being identical twins has caused us to rebel against all things cookie cutter, so we like to make things interesting. The webbed halter dress does just that. Even if you're wearing the same top, pants, or even bikini as everyone else, this dress will give you a unique edge. Get ready to stand out in the crowd!

finished size

S (M, L) sized to fit 30–32 (34–36, 38–40)" (76–81 [86.5–91.5, 96.5–101.5] cm) bust circumference.

finished measurements

About 34 (36, 38)" (86.5 [91.5, 96.5] cm) at waist (dress is extremely stretchy except at waistband).

yarn

Worsted weight (#4 Medium).

WE USED: Lily Sugar n' Cream (100% cotton; 95 yd [86 m]/2 oz [56 g]): 1 (1, 2) skein(s) #02743 summer splash (A), Red Heart Soft (100 % acrylic; 256 yd [234 m]/5 oz [140 g]): 1 (1, 2) skein(s) #2512 turquoise (B).

hook

Size H/8 (5 mm). Adjust hook size if necessary to obtain correct gauge.

notions

Removable marker; tapestry needle.

gauge

10 sc = 4" (10 cm) using A. Row gauge is not important for this project.

pattern notes

The halter top is worked back and forth in rows from the waist to the neck. The skirt begins with one row at the bottom of the waistband, and then the piece is joined to work in the round to the hem.

The remainder of the skirt is worked in a continuous spiral. Do not join rounds except as indicated. You may wish to use a marker to indicate the beginning of the round.

HALTER DRESS

TOP

Starting at the waistband and working toward neck, with B, ch 58 (62, 66).

ROW 1 (RS): Hdc in 3rd ch from hook (counts as 2 hdc) and in each rem ch across to end, turn—57 (61, 65).

Change to A.

ROW 2: Ch 2 (counts as hdc), hdc in each hdc across, turn.

ROW 3: Ch 3 (counts as dc), dc in next 2 (4, 6) hdc, * ch 10, sk next 5 hdc, dc in next hdc; rep from * across 7 more times, ch 10, sk next 5 hdc, dc in next 3 (5, 7) hdc, turn.

ROW 4: Ch 3 (counts as dc), sk next dc, dc in next 2 (4, 6), dc in next 5 chs, * ch 10, dc in center of next ch-10 lp; rep from * across to last ch-10 lp, sk next 5 chs, dc in next 5 chs, dc in next 3 (5, 7) dc, turn.

ROW 5: Ch 3 (counts as dc), sk first dc, dc in next 2 (4, 6) dc, ch 10, sk next 5 dc, * dc in center of next ch-10 lp; rep from * 7 more times, ch 10, sk next 5 dc, dc in last 3 (5, 7) dc, turn.

ROWS 6 AND 7: Rep Rows 4 and 5.

Fasten off. Weave in end.

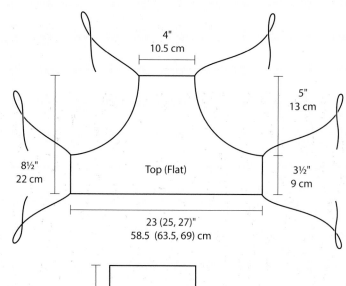

4"
10.5 cm

5"
13 cm

8½"
22 cm

Top (Flat)

3½"
9 cm

23 (25, 27)"
58.5 (63.5, 69) cm

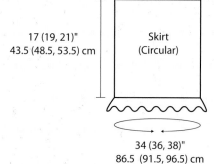

17 (19, 21)"
43.5 (48.5, 53.5) cm

Skirt
(Circular)

Dimensions are approximate, fabric is extremely stretchy.

34 (36, 38)"
86.5 (91.5, 96.5) cm

TOP TIES

Ch 52, hdc in beg ch-3 of Row 7, hdc in next 2 dc, * hdc in next 10 chs, hdc in next dc; rep from * 3 more times, ch 52. Fasten off. Weave in end. Repeat on other side of halter top.

SKIRT

With WS facing, join A to first ch of foundation ch.

ROW 1 (WS): Ch 3 (counts as dc), dc in next 2 (4, 6) chs, * ch 10, sk next 5 chs, dc in next ch; rep from * another 7 times, dc in last 3 (5, 7) chs, turn.

RND 2 (RS): Ch 3 (counts as dc), dc in next 2 (4, 6) dc, dc in next 5 chs, * ch 10, dc in next ch-10 lp; rep from * across to last ch-10 lp, ch 10, sk next 5 chs, dc in last 5 chs, dc in next 3 (5, 7) dc, do not turn, ch 24 (mark first ch and last ch); join with sl st in top of beg ch-3 of Rnd 2.

RND 3: Ch 3 (counts as dc), dc in next 2 (4, 6) dc, * ch 10, dc in center of next ch-10 lp; rep from * another 6 times, ch 10, sk next 5 dc, dc in next 3 (5, 7) dc, ** ch 10, sk next 5 chs, dc in next ch; rep from ** another 3 times.

RNDS 4–11 (13, 15): * Ch 10, dc in center of next ch-10 lp; rep from * around.

RUFFLE HEM

RND 1: Ch 2 (counts as hdc), hdc in each ch and dc around.

Change to B.

RND 2: Ch 2 (counts as hdc), hdc around.

Change to A.

RND 3: Ch 3 (counts as dc), 2 dc in same hdc, 3 dc in each hdc around; join with sl st in top of beg ch-3.

Fasten off. Weave in end.

BACK TIES

Ch 50, 2 hdc in first marked ch of Rnd 2 of bottom, hdc in each ch across to second marked st, ch 50. Fasten off. Weave in end.

tubeapron top
WITH LACING

This piece is part tube top, part dress, and all fabulous! You can wear this top over jeans or leggings, alone, or layered with a baby tee or a tailored jacket. The lacing makes it adjustable and versatile. Wear the lacing in the back for a corset look or even off to one side for a different take. The color blocks add visual interest while creating a slimming effect through the torso. What more could you want?

finished size
XS (S, M, L) sized to fit 26–28 (30–32, 34–36, 38–40)" (66–71.5 [76–81, 86.5–91.5, 96.5–101.5] cm) bust circumference.

finished measurements
20 (24, 28, 32)" (51 [61 71.5, 81.5] cm) in circumference by 34 (34, 35, 35)" (86.5 [86.5, 89, 89] cm) long. Actual circumference is determined by lacing.

yarn
Worsted weight (#4 Medium).

WE USED: Patons Classic Wool (100% wool; 223 yd [205 m]/3½ oz [100 g]): 1 (1, 2, 2) skeins #77414 rosewood (A), Red Heart Soft (100% acrylic, 256 yd [234 m]/5 oz [140 g]): 1 (1, 2, 2) skeins each #9537 fuchsia (B) and #1889 toast (C). MediumTLC Amore (80% acrylic, 20% nylon; 278 yd [254 m]/6 oz [170 g]): 1 (1, 2, 2) skeins #3908 raspberry (D).

hook
Size I/9 (5.5 mm). Adjust hook size if necessary to obtain correct gauge.

notions
Removable markers; tapestry needle; 2 decorative buttons, beads, or shells.

gauge
12 hdc and 12 rows = 4" (10 cm) using A.

APRON TOP

Starting at top, with A, ch 61 (73, 85, 97).

ROW 1 (RS): Hdc in 3rd ch from hook (counts as 2 hdc) and in each ch across to end, turn—60 (72, 84, 96) hdc. Mark first and last hdc.

ROWS 2–19 (2–19, 2–21, 2–21): Ch 2 (counts as hdc), hdc in each hdc across, turn.

Change to B.

ROWS 20–29 (20–29, 22–31, 22–31): Ch 1, sc in each hdc across to the end, turn.

Change to C.

ROW 30 (30, 32, 32): Ch 3 (counts as dc), dc in next 2 sc, * ch 1, sk next sc, dc in next sc; rep from * across to last 3 sc, dc in next 3 sc, turn.

ROWS 31–34 (31–34, 33–36, 33–36): Ch 3 (counts as dc), dc in next 2 dc, * ch 1, dc in next ch-1 sp; rep from * across to last 3 dc, dc in last 3 dc, turn.

Continue in patt as est, changing colors as foll:

Change to D, work 5 rows.

Change to A, work 5 rows.

Change to B, work 7 rows.

Change to C, work 7 rows.

Change to D, work 8 rows.

NEXT ROW: Ch 3 (counts as dc), dc in each dc and ch-1 sp across to end.

NEXT ROW: Ch 3 (counts as dc), dc in each dc across to end.

Fasten off. Weave in ends.

TRIM

LEFT SIDE EDGE

ROW 1 (RS): Join D to marked st of Row 1 of Apron, ch 3 (counts as dc), dc evenly across end of Rows to corner, turn.

ROW 2: Ch 3 (counts as dc), dc in each dc across to end.

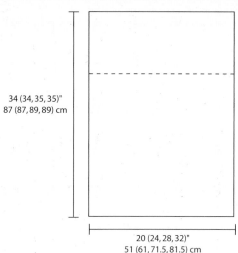

34 (34, 35, 35)"
87 (87, 89, 89) cm

20 (24, 28, 32)"
51 (61, 71.5, 81.5) cm

Fasten off. Weave in end.

RIGHT SIDE EDGE

ROW 1 (WS): Join D to marked st of Row 1, ch 3 (counts as dc), dc evenly across end of rows to corner, turn.

ROW 2: Ch 3 (counts as dc), dc in each dc across to end, do not turn.

TOP EDGE

Change to C.

ROW 1 (RS): Working across top edge of Apron, ch 2 (counts as hdc), hdc in each dc across to end, do not turn.

LEFT EDGE EYELETS

Change to B.

ROW 1 (RS): Ch 2 (counts as hdc), hdc in each hdc across to end, turn.

ROW 2: Ch 2 (counts as hdc), hdc in next 49 hdc, * ch 2, sk next hdc, hdc in next 4 hdc; rep from * another 11 times, ch 2, sk next hdc, sl st in next hdc.

Fasten off. Weave in end.

BOTTOM TRIM

ROW 1 (RS): Join B to first st of Row 1 for Left Edge Eyelets, working along bottom edge of Apron, ch 3 (counts as dc), sk next hdc, dc in next 2 hdc, * dc in next hdc, 3 dc in next hdc; rep from * across to last 4 sts leaving rem st unworked, do not turn.

RIGHT EDGE EYELETS

ROW 1 (RS): Working up right edge of Apron, hdc in each hdc across to end, turn.

ROW 2: Ch 3 (counts as hdc), sk first 2 hdc, * ch 2, sk next hdc, hdc in next 4 hdc; rep from * another 11 times, hdc across to bottom edge, sl st in next st.

Fasten off. Weave in end.

Lightly block apron top.

TIE

With C, ch 350. Fasten off. Weave in end. Sew 1 button, bead, or shell to each end of tie. Weave tie through Eyelets in crisscross pattern starting at top. Tie into bow at bottom eyelet.

hiphanger

This versatile little accessory can be worn just about any way you please! Add a splash of color to your outfit by simply draping the hip hanger over one hip. Try wearing it like an apron over jeans for an alternative to the dress-over-pants look.

finished size

S (M, L), sized to fit 31–34 (36–38, 40–43)" (78.7–83.4 [91.4–96.5, 101.6–109.2] cm) hip circumference.

finished measurements

36 (37, 38)" (91.5 [94, 96.5] cm) at widest point, unstretched (will stretch) and 18" (45.7 cm) long.

yarn

Worsted weight (#4 Medium).

WE USED: Berroco Boho (48% nylon, 25% cotton, 27% rayon; 98 yd [90 m]/ 1¾ oz [50 g]): 5 (5, 6) skeins #9272 torrero.

hook

Size G/6 (4 mm). Adjust hook size if necessary to obtain correct gauge.

gauge

16 dc and 8 rows = 4" (10 cm).

HIP HANGER

TIES

Ch 144 (148, 152).

ROW 1 (RS): Hdc in 3rd ch from hook (counts as 2 hdc) and in each ch across, turn—143 (147, 151) hdc.

ROW 2: Ch 3 (counts as dc), dc in next 4 (6, 8) hdc, * ch 1, sk next hdc, dc in next 3 hdc; rep from * across to last 2 (4, 6) hdc, dc in last 2 (4, 6) hdc, turn.

ROW 3: Ch 3 (counts as dc), dc in next 3 (5, 7) dc, * ch 1, sk next dc, dc in next ch-1 sp, dc in next 2 dc; rep from * across to last 3 (5, 7) dc, dc in last 3 (5, 7) dc, turn.

ROW 4: Ch 3 (counts as dc), dc in next 4 (6, 8) dc, * ch 1, sk next dc, dc in next ch-1 sp, dc in next 2 dc; rep from * across to last 2 (4, 6) dc, dc in last 2 (4, 6) dc, turn.

ROW 5: Ch 3 (counts as dc), dc in next 2 (4, 6) dc, * ch 1, sk next dc, dc in next dc, ch 1, sk next ch-1 sp, dc in next dc; rep from * across to last 2 (4, 6) dc, dc in last 2 (4, 6) dc, turn.

SKIRT

ROW 6 (DECREASE ROW): Ch 1, sl st in next 38 (39, 40) sts, ch 3 (counts as dc), dc in next

66 (68, 70) sts, turn leaving rem 38 (39, 40) sts unworked—67 (69, 71) dc.

ROW 7 (RS): Ch 3 (counts as dc), dc in next 2 (3, 4) dc, * ch 1, sk next dc, dc in next dc; rep from * across to last 2 (3, 4) dc, dc in last 2 (3, 4) dc, turn.

ROW 8: Ch 3 (counts as dc), dc in next 3 (4, 5) dc, dc in next ch-1 sp, * ch 1, dc in next ch-1 sp; rep from * across to last 3 (4, 5) dc, dc in last 3 (4, 5) dc.

ROW 9: Ch 3 (counts as dc), dc in next 2 (3, 4) dc, * ch 1; dc in next ch-1 sp rep from * across to last 2 (3, 4) dc, ch 1, sk next dc, dc in last 2 (3, 4) dc, turn.

ROWS 10–12: Rep Rows 8 and 9, then repeat Row 8 once more.

ROW 13: Ch 3 (counts as dc), dc in next 4 (5, 6) dc, * ch 1, sk next dc, dc in next ch-1 sp, dc in next dc, dc in next ch-1 sp; rep from * across to last 2 (3, 4) dc, dc in last 2 (3, 4) dc.

ROW 14: Ch 3 (counts as dc), dc in next 4 (5, 6) dc, * ch 1, sk next ch-1 sp, dc in next 3 dc; rep from * across to last 2 (3, 4) dc, dc in last 2 (3, 4) dc, turn.

ROWS 15–22: Rep Rows 7–14.

ROWS 23–27: Rep Rows 7–11.

ROW 28: Ch 3 (counts as dc), dc in each dc and ch-1 sp across, turn.

ROW 29: Ch 3 (counts as dc), dc in next 4 (5, 6) dc, * ch 1, sk next dc, dc in next 3 dc; rep from * across to last 2 (3, 4) dc, dc in last 2 (3, 4) dc, turn.

ROW 30: Ch 3 (counts as dc), dc in next 4 (5, 6) dc * ch 1, sk next ch-1 sp or dc, [dc in next ch-1 sp or dc] twice; rep from * across to last 5 (6, 7) dc, dc in last 5 (6, 7) dc, turn.

ROW 31: Ch 3 (counts as dc), dc in next 7 (8, 9) dc, * ch 1, sk next ch-1 sp, dc in next 2 dc; rep from * across to last 3 (4, 5) dc, dc in last 3 (4, 5) dc, turn.

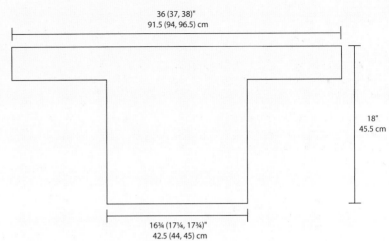

36 (37, 38)"
91.5 (94, 96.5) cm

18"
45.5 cm

16¾ (17¼, 17¾)"
42.5 (44, 45) cm

ROW 32: Ch 3 (counts as dc), dc in next 4 (5, 6) dc, * ch 1, sk next ch-1 sp, dc in next 2 dc; rep from * across to last 5 (6, 7) dc, dc in last 5 (6, 7) dc, turn.

ROWS 33 AND 34: Rep Rows 31 and 32.

ROW 35: Ch 3 (counts as dc), dc in each dc and ch-1 sp across, turn.

ROWS 36–38: Ch 3 (counts as dc), dc in next 6 (7, 8) dc, * ch 1, sk next dc, dc in next dc; rep from * across to last 5 (6, 7) dc, dc in last 5 (6, 7) dc, turn.

ROW 39: Ch 3 (counts as dc), dc in each dc and ch-1 sp across.

ROW 40: Rep Row 7. If desired, continue in patt as est to lengthen skirt.

Do not fasten off.

TRIM

With RS facing, sc evenly around entire piece working 3 sc in each corner st. Fasten off. Weave in end.

Lightly block hip hanger to dimensions.

remixt-shirt

SLEEVES

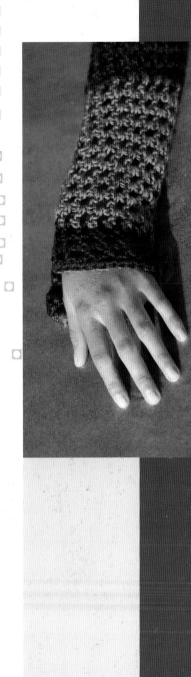

Have you ever had a shirt that fits you just right? That perfect T-shirt that you just love—but let's face it, is a little plain? Well, we have the perfect solution—crocheted sleeves! These sleeves are a quick and easy way to let your personal style shine through.

finished size
Determined by the T-shirt size.

finished measurments
About 20" (51 cm) long, made to match circumference of T-shirt sleeve.

yarn
Worsted weight (#4 Medium).
WE USED: Caron Simply Soft (100% acrylic, 165 yd [151 m]/3 oz [85 g])): 1 hank each #2680 black (A), #2721 autumn red (B), #2714 copper kettle (discontinued) (C), #2722 chocolate (D).

hook
Size G/6 (4 mm). Adjust hook size if necessary to obtain correct gauge.

notions
Removable markers; tapestry needle.

gauge
About 16 dc and 6 rows = 4" (10 cm), unstretched.

pattern notes

This sleeve is custom made to fit on any T-shirt, so there are no stitch counts in this pattern.

The sleeve is worked in a continuous spiral. Do not join rounds. You may wish to use a marker to indicate the beginning of the rnd.

SLEEVE

With a 14" (36 cm) strand of A and tapestry needle, weave yarn in and out of T-shirt sleeve edge forming ½" (1.25 cm) loops evenly spaced around. Fasten off. Tie ends tog.

RND 1: Join A to lp at underarm, ch 3 (counts as dc), 2 dc in same lp, * 3 dc in each lp; rep from * around.

RND 2: Dc in each dc around.

Count your stitches. If you don't have an even number, work another dc in the same stitch as the prev st to increase 1.

RND 3: *Ch 1, sk next dc, dc in next dc; rep from * around.

RND 4: * Ch 1, dc in next ch-1 sp; rep from * around.

Continue to work in spiral rounds in patt as est changing colors as foll:

With A, work 5 more rnds.

Change to B, work 5 rnds.

Change to C, work 10 rnds.

Change to D, work 4 rnds. To elongate sleeves, continue in patt as est to desired length.

RND 31: Hdc in each dc and ch-1 sp around; join with sl st in first hdc.

Fasten off. Weave in end.

Rep for second sleeve.

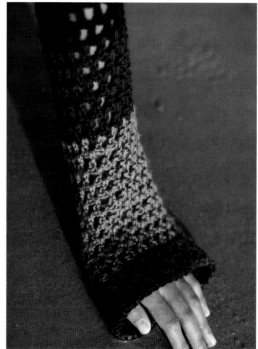

funkyone sleeve

WITH WRAPAROUND TIES

Once upon a time there were two sisters that loved to crochet, but they refused to create anything conventional. . . . So the Funky One Sleeve was born! Since most of us usually think of sleeves as coming in pairs, we thought we'd make just one sleeve that can be added to a tube top or your favorite sleeveless dress. Go asymmetrical in an unexpected way and have fun coming up with new ways to tie on the wraparound laces.

finished size
S (M, L) sized to fit 8–10 (10–12, 12–14)" (20.5–25.5 [25.5–30.5, 30.5–36] cm) upper arm circumference.

finished measurements
About 9 (10½, 12)" [23 (27, 30.5) cm] in circumference and 24" (61 cm) long (unstretched).

yarn
Worsted weight (#4 Medium).

WE USED: TLC Cotton Plus (51% cotton, 49% acrylic; 178 yd [162.7 m]/3½ oz [100 g]): 1 ball #3252 tangerine (A) and 1 ball #3303 tan (B).

hook
Size G/6 (4.25 mm). Adjust hook size if necessary to obtain correct gauge.

notions
Removable markers; tapestry needle.

gauge
16 dc and 6 rows = 4" (10 cm).

pattern note

Sleeve is worked in a continuous spiral. Do not join rounds except as indicated. You may wish to use a removable marker to indicate the beginning of the round.

SLEEVE

Start at cuff and work up toward shoulder.

With A, ch 36 (42, 48). Join with sl st to first ch to form circle, being careful not to twist.

RND 1: Ch 3 (counts as dc), sk next ch, dc in each ch around, dc in top ch of beg ch-3 to join—36 (42, 48) dc.

RND 2: * Ch 1, sk next dc, dc in next 2 dc; rep from * around.

RNDS 3–11: * Ch 1, sk ch-1 sp, dc in next 2 dc; rep from * around.

Change to B.

RNDS 12–21: * Ch 1, sk ch sp, dc in next 2 dc; rep from *.

RND 22: Hdc in each dc and ch-1 sp around.

RND 23: Hdc around.

Change to A.

RND 24: Hdc around.

Change to B.

RND 25: Hdc around.

Change to A.

RND 26: * Dc in next hdc, ch 1, sk next hdc; rep from * ending with ch 1, sk last hdc.

RND 27: Dc in next dc, * dc in next ch-1 sp, ch 1; rep from * around.

RND 28: Sk first 2 dc, * dc in next ch-1 sp, ch 1; rep from * around.

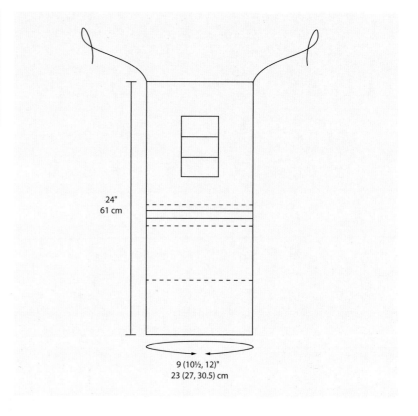

24"
61 cm

9 (10½, 12)"
23 (27, 30.5) cm

RND 29: [Dc in next ch-1 sp, ch 1] twice, [dc in next ch-1 sp, dc in next dc] twice, ch 10, sk next 5 ch-1 sp, dc in next dc, dc in next ch-1 sp, dc in next dc, *ch 1, dc in next ch-1 sp; rep from * to end of rnd.

RND 30: [Ch 1, dc in next ch-1 sp] twice, ch 1, sk next dc, dc in next 3 dc, ch 10, sk ch-10 lp, dc in next 3 dc, dc in next ch-1 sp, * ch 1, dc in next ch-1 sp; rep from * to end of rnd.

RND 31: [Ch 1, dc in next ch-1 sp] 3 times, dc in next 3 dc, ch 10, sk ch-10 lp, dc in next 3 dc, *ch 1, dc in next ch-1 sp; rep from * to end of rnd.

RND 32: [Ch 1, dc in next ch-1 sp] 3 times, ch 1, sk next dc, dc in next 3 dc, dc in next 10 chs, dc in next 3 dc, dc in next ch-1 sp, * ch 1, dc in next ch-1 sp; rep from * to end of rnd.

RND 33: [Ch 1, dc in next ch-1 sp] 4 times, ch 1, sk next dc, dc in next 16 dc, * ch 1, dc in next ch-1 sp; rep from * to end of rnd.

RND 34: [Ch 1, dc in next ch-1 sp] 4 times, ch 1, sk next dc, dc in next 15 dc, dc in next ch-1 sp, *ch 1, dc in next ch-1 sp; rep from * to end of rnd.

RND 35: [Ch 1, dc in next ch-1 sp] 5 times, [ch 1, sk next dc, dc in next dc] 8 times, *ch 1, dc in next ch-1 sp; rep from * to end of rnd.

RNDS 36–38: * Ch 1, sk next dc, dc in next ch-1 sp; rep from * around.

RND 39: Hdc in each dc and ch-1 sp around. Mark 10th (12th, 14th) and 29th (31st, 33rd) st.

Fasten off. Weave in ends.

Lightly block sleeve.

TIES

(MAKE 2)

With A, ch 150. Fasten off. Sew one tie to each marked st of last rnd. Weave in ends.

hooded poncho
WITH BOOT COVERS

We've always been dedicated to making clothes that flatter the feminine silhouette. Believe it or not, we've found a way to do just that with a poncho! With the addition of lacing in the back, we've given you the freedom to transform this hooded poncho into a fitted top. You can cinch in the waist or let it hang loose. Add the sleek matching boot covers and head out to grab a coffee.

finished size

PONCHO: one size (with adjustable ties) fits 30–40" (76–101.5] cm) bust circumference.

BOOT COVER: S (M, L) to fit over women's boots sizes 4–6 (7–9, 10–11) (with adjustable lacing).

finished measurements

PONCHO: 28" (71.5 cm) long from neckline to hem at center front.

BOOT COVER: About 12 (13,14½)" (30.5 [33, 37] cm) in circumference (exact size is determined by lacing).

yarn

Chunky weight (#5 Bulky).

WE USED: Lion Brand Wool-Ease Chunky (80% acrylic, 20% wool; 153 yd [140 m]/5 oz [140 g]): #630-130 grass (A), 3 balls for Poncho and 1 (1, 2) balls for Boot Covers, Lion Brand Lion Suede (100% polyester; 122 yd [110 m]/3 oz [85 g]): #210-178 teal (B), 1 ball is enough to work Poncho and Boot Covers.

hook

Size H/8 (5 mm). Adjust hook size if necessary to obtain correct gauge.

notions

Removable markers; tapestry needle; 2 decorative buttons or beads.

gauge

11 dc and 6 rows = 4" (10 cm) using A.

BOOT COVER

(MAKE 2)

With A, ch 28 (32, 36).

ROW 1: Dc in 4th ch from hook (counts as 2 dc) and in each ch across, turn—26 (30, 34) dc.

ROWS 2–5 (2–5, 2–6): Ch 3 (counts as dc), dc in each dc across to end, turn.

Change to B.

ROW 6 (6, 7): Ch 2 (counts as hdc), hdc in each dc across to end, turn.

Change to A.

ROW 7 (7, 8): Ch 3 (counts as dc), dc in each of next 22 (26, 30) sts leaving rem sts unworked, turn—23 (27, 31) dc.

ROWS 8–13 (8–14, 9–16): Ch 3 (counts as dc), dc in each dc across to end, turn.

Change to B.

ROW 14 (15, 17): Ch 2 (counts as hdc), hdc across, turn.

Change to A.

ROW 15 (16, 18): Ch 3 (counts as dc), dc in each of next 18 (22, 26) dc leaving rem sts unworked, turn—19 (23, 27) dc.

ROWS 15–18 (16–19, 18–22): Ch 3 (counts as dc), dc in each dc across to end, turn.

ROW 19 (20, 23): Ch 3 (counts as dc), dc in each dc across to end.

Fasten off. Weave in end.

TRIM

With A, ch 34 (35, 41).

ROW 1: Dc in 4th ch from hook (counts as 2 dc) and in each ch across, turn—32 (35, 39) dc.

ROWS 2–4 (2–5, 2–6): Ch 3 (counts as dc), dc in each dc across to end, turn.

Change to B.

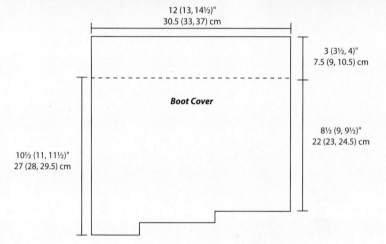

12 (13, 14½)"
30.5 (33, 37) cm

3 (3½, 4)"
7.5 (9, 10.5) cm

Boot Cover

8½ (9, 9½)"
22 (23, 24.5) cm

10½ (11, 11½)"
27 (28, 29.5) cm

ROW 5 (6, 7): Ch 2 (counts as hdc), hdc in each dc across to end, turn.

Change to A.

ROW 6 (7, 8): Ch 3 (counts as dc), dc in each dc across to end.

Fasten off. Weave in end. Sew last row across ends of rows on straight edge of Boot Cover.

BORDER

With RS facing, attach B to uneven edge of Boot Cover. Ch 1, hdc evenly across ends of rows. Do not turn. Change to A. Ch 2, *hdc in next 2 sts, ch 1, sk next st, hdc in next 3 sts; rep from * evenly across side of Boot Cover. Work hdc evenly across straight end of Boot Cover. Ch 2, *hdc in next 2 sts, ch 1, sk next st, hdc in next 3 sts; rep from * evenly across second side of Boot Cover. Join with sl st to top of ch-2. Fasten off. Weave in end.

TIE

With B, ch 50, sl st across to edge of trim, ch 50. Fasten off.

Lace chain just made through the ch-1 sps of border in crisscross pattern like shoelaces. Tie in bow at top.

PONCHO

With A, ch 177. Mark 69th and 108th stitch.

(B)PANEL 1

ROW 1 (RS): Dc in 4th ch from hook (counts as 2 dc), dc in next 4 chs, * ch 1, sk next ch, dc in next 2 chs; rep from * across to last 4 chs, dc in last 4 chs, turn—175 sts.

ROWS 2–4: Ch 3 (counts as dc), dc in next 5 dc, * ch 1, sk next ch-1 sp, dc in next 2 dc; rep from * across to last 4 dc, dc in last 4 dc, turn.

Change to B.

ROW 5: Ch 1, sc in each dc and ch across to end, turn.

PANEL 2

ROW 6 (WS): Sl st in next 4 sc, change to A, ch 3 (counts as dc), dc in next 5 sc, * ch 1, sk next sc, dc in next sc; rep from * across to last 9 sc, dc in next 5 sc leaving rem 4 sts unworked, turn—167 sts rem.

ROWS 7–9: Ch 3 (counts as dc), dc in next 5 dc, * ch 1, sk next ch-1 sp, dc in next dc; rep from * across to last 5 dc, dc in last 5 dc, turn.

Change to B.

ROW 10: Ch 1, sc in each dc across to end, turn.

PANEL 3

ROW 11 (RS): Sl st in next 5 sc, change to A, ch 3 (counts as dc), dc in next 6 sc, * ch 3, sk next 3 sc, dc in next 2 sc; rep from * across to last 10 sc, dc in next 5 sc leaving rem 5 sts unworked, turn—157 sts rem.

ROWS 12–14: Ch 3 (counts as dc), dc in next 6 dc, * ch 3, sk next ch-3 lp, dc in next 2 dc; rep from * across to last 7 dc, dc in next dc, turn.

Change to B.

ROW 15: Ch 1, sc in each dc across to end, turn.

PANEL 4

ROW 16 (WS): Sl st in next 7 sc, change to A, ch 3 (counts as dc), dc in next 6 sc, * ch 5, sk next 2 sc, dc in next sc; rep from * across to last 14 sc, dc in next 7 sc leaving rem 7 sts unworked for now, turn—143 sts rem.

ROW 17: Ch 3 (counts as dc), dc in next 6 dc, 2 dc in next ch-5 lp, * ch 5, dc in next ch-5 lp; rep from * across to last ch-5 lp, 2 dc in ch-5 lp, dc in last 7 dc, turn.

ROW 18: Ch 3 (counts as dc), dc in next 6 dc, * ch 5, dc in next ch-5 lp; rep from * across to last 9 dc, sk next 2 dc, dc in next 7 dc, turn.

ROW 19: Rep Row 17.

Fasten off. Weave in end.

Fold piece in half lengthwise, with RS tog, sl st the first and last 14" (36 cm) of Row 1 tog for center front seam.

HOOD
(MAKE 2)

With A, ch 39.

ROW 1: Dc in 4th ch from hook (counts as 2 dc), dc in next 3 chs, * ch 1, sk next ch, dc in next ch; rep from * across to last 4 chs, dc in next 4 chs, turn—38 sts.

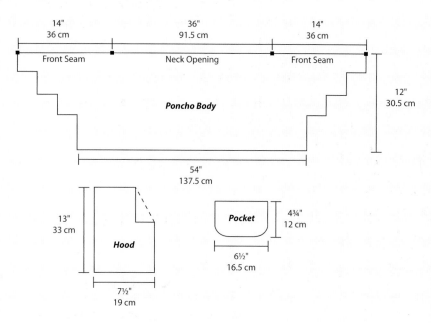

Poncho Body

14"
36 cm — Front Seam

36"
91.5 cm — Neck Opening

14"
36 cm — Front Seam

12"
30.5 cm

54"
137.5 cm

13"
33 cm

Hood

7½"
19 cm

Pocket

4¾"
12 cm

6½"
16.5 cm

ROW 2: Ch 3 (counts as dc), dc in next 4 dc, dc in next ch-1 sp, * ch 1, sk next dc, dc in next ch-1 sp; rep from * across to last 5 dc, dc in next 5 dc, turn.

ROW 3: Ch 3 (counts as dc), dc in next 4 dc, *ch 1, sk next dc, dc in next ch-1 sp; rep from * across to last 6 dc, ch, skip 1 dc, dc in next 5 dc, turn.

ROW 4–11: Rep Rows 2 and 3 another 4 times.

ROW 12: Ch 3 (counts as dc), dc in each dc and ch-1 sp across, turn.

Fold corner of piece over to WS as shown in diagram above and stitch in place. This will be top back corner of hood. Place hood pieces with WS tog and sl st around back and top edges, leaving bottom and front open.

Sl st hood to poncho between marked sts of Row 1 of poncho.

POCKET

Starting at top, with A, ch 19.

ROW 1: Dc in 4th ch from hook (counts as 2 dc) and in each ch across, turn—17 dc.

ROW 2: Ch 3 (counts as dc), dc in each dc across to end, turn.

ROW 3: Ch 3 (counts as dc), dc2tog, dc across to last 2 dc, dc2tog, turn.

ROW 4: Ch 3 (counts as dc), dc in each dc across to end, turn.

ROWS 5 and **6:** Rep Rows 3 and 4.

ROW 7: Ch 3 (counts as dc), dc2tog, dc across to last 2 dc, dc2tog, turn.

Change to B.

RND 8: Ch 1, sc evenly around entire pocket working 3 sc in top corners.

Fasten off. Weave in end.

Sew 3 sides of pocket to bottom center front of poncho.

FINISHING

OUTSIDE EDGE TRIM: Join B to outside edge of Poncho at any point, ch1, sc evenly around entire outside edge of poncho. When you come to the section with the chain spaces, work 4 sc in each ch sp and 1 sc in each dc between the ch spaces. Join with sl st to ch 1 at beg of rnd. Fasten off. Weave in end.

FRONT OPENING TRIM: Join A to inside edge of Poncho at top of center front seam. Ch1, work hdc evenly around entire front opening of poncho and hood, join with sl st to ch 1 at beg of rnd. Change to B, ch 1 and work sc evenly around entire neck edge, join with sl st to ch at beg of rnd. Fasten off. Weave in end.

HOOD TIE (MAKE 2): With B, ch 33 (35, 37). Fasten off. Slip button or bead over end. Tie end into a knot. Sew opposite end of tie to bottom corner of hood.

PONCHO TIE: With B, ch 58 (60, 62). Fasten off. Slip one end through each edge of poncho at waist level. Tie in bow.

Lightly block all pieces.

beachbikini

TOP AND SKIRT

This summer ensemble is perfect for a picnic at the beach or an afternoon by the pool. The pieces also work as mix-and-match separates. Try the bikini top with a skirt or jeans for a flirty outfit, and the skirt works nicely as a lightweight bikini bottom cover-up. The crochet loop trim at the skirt hem is a versatile detail that can be added to just about any crochet project.

finished size

TOP: XS (S, M, L) sized to fit 26–28 (30–32, 34–36, 38–40)" (66–71.1 [76–81, 86.5–91.5, 96.5–101.5] cm) with A/B cup bust circumference.

SKIRT: XS (S,M,L) sized to fit 29–30 (31–34, 36–38, 40–43)" (73.6–76.2 [78.7–83.4, 91.4–96.5, 101.6–109.2] cm) waist circumference.

finished measurements

TOP: 13½ (15¾, 18, 20¼)" (34.3 [40, 45.7, 51.4 cm) across front (circumference is determined by tying).

SKIRT: 31 (35½, 40, 44½)" (78.7 [90.1, 101.6, 113] cm) in circumference at hip and 23 (26½, 30, 33½)" (58.4 [67.3, 76.2, 85] cm) at waist (waist is not very stretchy, so make a size that is large enough to pull on over your hips).

yarn

Worsted weight (#4 Medium).

WE USED: Bernat Cool Crochet (70% cotton, 30% nylon; 200 yd [182 m]/1¾ oz [50 g]): 5 (6, 6, 7) skeins #74131 denim (A), 3 (4, 4, 5) skeins #74130 tie-dye shades (B), 1 skein #74008 summer cream (C).

hook

Size H/8 (5 mm). Adjust hook size if necessary to obtain correct gauge. Size J/10 (6 mm) hook for waistband and ties on skirt.

notions

Removable markers; tapestry needle.

gauge

14 sc and 20 rows = 4" (10 cm) for top, using a double strand of yarn.
14 dc and 7 rows = 4" (10 cm) for skirt, using a double strand of yarn.

BIKINI TOP

With 2 strands of B held tog and smaller hook, ch 47 (55, 63, 71).

ROW 1 (RS): Sc in 2nd ch from hook and in each ch across, turn—46 (54, 62, 70) sc.

ROWS 2–4: Ch 1, sc across, turn.

Change to A.

ROW 5: Ch 2 (counts as hdc), hdc across, turn.

ROW 6: Ch 1, sc across, turn.

Do not fasten off.

FIRST CUP

Change to B.

ROW 7: Ch 1, sc in next 23 (27, 31, 35) hdc, turn leaving rem 23 (27, 31, 35) hdc unworked.

ROWS 8–13 (13, 15): Ch 1, sc across, turn.

NEXT ROW (WS, DECREASE ROW): Ch 1, sc2tog, sc across to last 2 sc, sc2tog, turn—21 (25, 29, 33) sc.

NEXT ROW (RS): Ch 1, sc across, turn.

Rep last 2 rows until 3 sc rem, end after completing a RS row.

Ch 41 (45, 49, 54). Fasten off. Weave in end.

SECOND CUP

With RS facing, join 2 strands of B to first skipped st of Row 6. Work as for First Cup until 3 sts rem, end after completing a WS row.

Ch 41 (45, 49, 54). Fasten off. Weave in end.

TRIM AND TIES

SIDE TRIM AND TOP TIES: With RS facing, join 2 strands of A to bottom right corner of top, sc along outer ends of rows evenly across to top corner st of piece, ch 41 (45, 49, 54). Fasten off. Weave in end.

With 2 strands of B, ch 41 (45, 49, 54), with RS facing, beg at top left edge of piece, sc along outer ends of rows evenly across to bottom corner st of piece. Fasten off. Weave in end.

BOTTOM TIES: With 2 strands of A, ch 66 (70, 74, 78), with RS facing, sc in first ch of foundation ch, sc in each ch across, ch 64 (70, 74, 78). Fasten off. Weave in end.

SIDE TIES (MAKE 2): With B, ch 66 (70, 74, 78). Fasten off. Sew ties to outside edges of top at bottom of cups.

FRONT TRIM: With RS facing, join a single strand of C to the inside top corner of First Cup. Working along ends of rows, sc evenly down center of piece and up to top corner of Second Cup. Fasten off. Weave in end. Sew front trim tog between cups at center up about 5 rows. Fasten off.

---

pattern note

The body of the skirt is worked in a continuous spiral. Do not join rounds except as indicated. You may wish to use a marker to indicate the beginning of the round.

SKIRT

With 2 strands of A and smaller hook, ch 108 (124, 140, 156), join with sl st to form ring.

RND 1: Ch 3 (counts as dc), dc in each ch around—108 (124, 140, 156) dc.

RNDS 2 AND 3: Dc around.

Change to B.

RNDS 4–12: Dc around.

Change to A.

RND 13: * Ch 1, sk next dc, dc in next dc; rep from * around.

RNDS 14–18: * Ch 1, dc in next ch-1 sp; rep from * around.

Turn and beg working back and forth to create slit as foll:

ROWS 19–21 (23, 25, 27): Ch 3 (counts as dc), dc in next ch-1 sp, *ch 1, dc in next ch-1 sp; rep from * around to last ch-1 sp, dc in last ch-1 sp, turn.

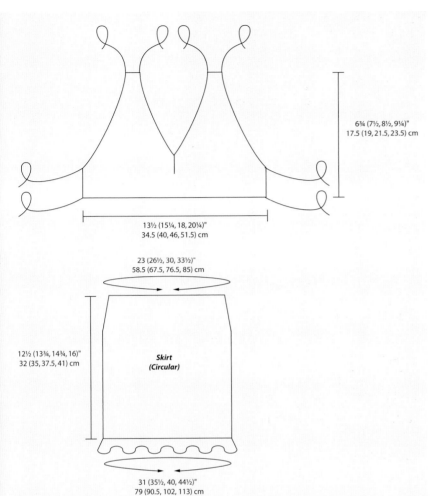

6¾ (7½, 8½, 9¼)"
17.5 (19, 21.5, 23.5) cm

13½ (15¼, 18, 20¼)"
34.5 (40, 46, 51.5) cm

23 (26½, 30, 33½)"
58.5 (67.5, 76.5, 85) cm

12½ (13¾, 14¾, 16)"
32 (35, 37.5, 41) cm

Skirt
(Circular)

31 (35½, 40, 44½)"
79 (90.5, 102, 113) cm

RNDS 1 AND 2: Ch 2 (counts as hdc), hdc around—108 (124, 140, 156) hdc.

RND 3: Change to larger hook, * hdc in next 3 hdc, sk next hdc; rep from * around—81 (93, 105, 117) hdc. Join with sl st.

Fasten off. Weave in end.

TIES

FIRST TIE: With 1 strand of B and 1 strand of C held tog and larger hook, ch 70 (72, 76, 80), sc in any hdc of Rnd 3 of waistband, sc around to last 4 hdc, sk last 4 hdc for center front opening, ch 70 (72, 76, 80). Fasten off. Weave in end.

SECOND TIE: With 2 strands of A and larger hook, ch 70 (72, 76, 80), sc in first sc of first tie, sc in each sc of first tie, ch 70 (72, 76, 80). Fasten off. Weave in end.

THIRD TIE: With 1 strand of B and 1 strand of C held tog and larger hook, ch 70 (72, 76, 80), sc in first sc of second tie, sc in each sc of second tie, ch 70 (72, 76, 80). Fasten off. Weave in end.

Lightly block all pieces.

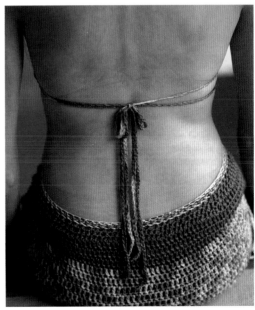

NEXT ROW: Ch 2 (counts as hdc), hdc in each dc and ch-1 sp across, turn.

Do not fasten off.

LOOP TRIM

ROW 1: * Ch 14, sc in next hdc; rep from * across.

Fasten off. Weave in end.

WAISTBAND

Join 2 strands of A to any ch of foundation ch with smaller hook.

overheadsleeves
WITH CONTRAST EDGING

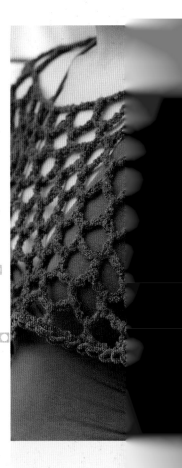

Have you ever wanted to feel covered up, but not really be all covered up? Well, that's the motivation behind the overhead sleeves. The open structure of the crochet makes these sleeves light and airy, providing a little bit of cover without going for a full sweater. These sleeves are perfect when you are right between tank top weather and pulling out those chunky winter sweaters.

finished size
S (M, L) sized to fit about 30–32 (34–36, 38–40)" (76–81 [86.5–91.5, 96.5–101.5] cm) bust circumference. This garment is worn very loosely and slips on easily over the head, so these sizes are only a guide. To determine the correct size, measure your arm span from wrist to wrist and refer to finished measurements below.

finished measurements
About 56 (60, 64)" (163 [173, 183] cm) from cuff to cuff. (This fabric is very stretchy and has a fluid drape.)

yarn
(A) Worsted weight (#4 Medium); (B) Chunky weight (# 5 Bulky).

WE USED: TLC Amore (80% acrylic, 20% nylon; 278 yd [254 m]/6 oz [170 g]): 1 (1, 2) skein(s) #3324 chocolate (A), Lion Brand Lion Suede (100% polyester;122 yd [110 m]/3 oz [85 g]): 1 (1, 2) skein(s) #210-1146 fuchsia (B).

hook
Size K/10 ½ (6.5 mm). Adjust hook size if necessary to obtain correct gauge.

notions
Removable markers; tapestry needle.

gauge
12 dc = 4" (10 cm) using A. Gauge is not crucial for this project.

SLEEVES

BACK

Starting at bottom and working toward top, with A, ch 135 (141, 147).

ROW 1 (RS): Dc in 4th ch from hook (counts as 2 hdc), dc in next 5 chs, * ch 5, sk next 2 chs, dc in next ch; rep from * across to last 6 chs, dc in last 6 chs, turn—40 (42, 44) ch 5 lps, 7 dc at each end for cuffs.

ROW 2: Ch 3 (counts as dc), dc next 3 dc, sk 3 dc, ch 5, * dc in center of next ch-5 lp, ch 5; rep from * across to last 7 dc, sk 3 dc, dc in last 4 dc, turn—41 (43, 45) ch 5 lps, 4 dc at each end.

ROW 3: Ch 3 (counts as dc), dc in next 3 dc, 3 dc in first ch-5 lp, * ch 5, dc in center of next ch-5 lp; rep from * across to last ch-5 lp, ch 5, 3 dc in next ch-5 lp, dc in next 4 dc, turn—40 (42, 44) ch 5 lps, 7 dc at each end.

ROWS 4–9: Rep Rows 2 and 3 another 3 times.

Do not fasten off.

NECK OPENING

Mark center 6 chain loops for neck opening.

ROW 10: Ch 3 (counts as dc), dc next 3 dc, sk 3 dc, ch 5, * dc in center of next ch-5 lp, ch 5; rep from * 17 times, ch 30 (neck opening), sk next 6 ch-5 lps, ** dc in center of next ch-5 lp, ch 5; rep from ** across to last 7 dc, sk 3 dc, dc in last 4 dc, turn.

ROW 11: Ch 3 (counts as dc), dc in next 3 dc, 3 dc in first ch-5 lp, * ch 5, dc in center of next ch-5 lp; rep from * across 16 times, ch 5, sk next 2 chs of ch-30 lp, dc in next ch, ** ch 5, sk next 3 chs; rep from ** across neck opening 5 times, ch 5, dc in next ch-5 lp; rep from * across to last ch-5 lp, ch 5, 3 dc in next ch-5 lp, dc in next 4 dc, turn—40 (42, 44) ch 5 lps, 7 dc at each end.

Do not fasten off.

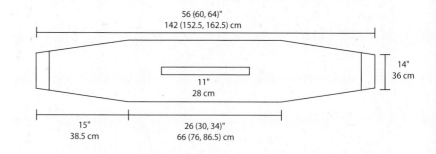

FRONT

ROWS 12–17: Rep Rows 2 and 3 another 3 times.

ROW 18: Rep Row 2 once more.

ROW 19: Ch 3 (counts as dc), dc in next 3 dc, 3 dc in first ch-5 lp, * ch 5, dc in center of next ch-5 lp; rep from * across to last ch-5 lp, 3 dc in next ch-5 lp, dc in last 4 dc.

Fasten off. Weave in end.

FINISHING

Starting at cuff, sl st 15" (38.5 cm) of Row 1 to Row 19 for underarm seam. Fasten off. Weave in end. Repeat on other end.

CUFF TRIM

With B, join yarn to cuff at seam.

RND 1: Sc evenly around opening.

RND 2: Sc in each sc around; join with sl st in beg sc.

Fasten off. Weave in end.

Rep on second sleeve.

BOTTOM TRIM: With B, join yarn to bottom opening at seam.

RND 1: Sc evenly around opening; join with sl st in beg sc.

Fasten off. Weave in end.

cropped sweater

WITH LACE-UP CLOSURE

So, it's time to pull out those sweaters for fall, but why not go with a cute cropped version instead? This cropped sweater gives you the option to create a layered look while still keeping you snug and warm. The combination of stitches in deep red and orange tones, punctuated by just a hint of brighter orange and purple creates a fantastic visual texture with a spicy color combo to match the changing leaves.

finished size

S (M, L) sized to fit 30–32 (34–36, 38–40)" (76–81 [86.5–91.5, 96.5–101.5] cm) bust circumference.

finished measurements

About 29 (32, 37)" (71 [79, 86] cm) bust circumference (exact circumference determined by tying).

yarn

Worsted weight (#4 Medium) (A,B,C); Chunky weight (#5 Bulky) (D).

WE USED: Caron Simply Soft (100% acrylic; 330 yd [303 m]/6 oz [127 g]): 2 (2, 3) skeins #9730 red (A), TLC Essentials (100% acrylic; 245 yd [224 m]/4½ oz [127 g]): 1 (2, 2) skeins #2918 harvest (B), Red Heart Soft (100% acrylic; 256 yd [234 m]/5 oz [127 g]): 1 (1, 2) skeins #9275 paprika (C), Lion Brand Lion Suede (100% polyester; 122 yd [112 m]/3 oz [85 g]): 1 (1, 1) skein #219-133 spice (D).

hook

Size I/9 (5.5 mm). Adjust hook size if necessary to obtain correct gauge.

notions

Removable markers; tapestry needle.

gauge

13 dc and 6 rows = 4" (10 cm).

SWEATER

SLEEVE

(MAKE 2)

Starting at bottom of sleeve and working toward top, with A, ch 37 (46, 55); join with sl st in first ch to form ring.

RND 1: Ch 3 (counts as dc), dc in each ch around—37 (46, 55) dc.

RNDS 2–5: Dc in each dc around.

RND 6: * Ch 1, sk next dc, dc in next 2 dc; rep from * around to last dc, ch 1, sk last dc.

RNDS 7–10: * Dc in next ch-1 sp, dc in next dc, ch 1, sk next dc; rep from * around to last dc, ch 1, sk last dc.

Change to B.

RND 11: Dc in each dc and ch-1 sp around.

RND 12: Dc in each dc around.

Change to C.

Work 5 Rnds in dc.

Rep Rnds 6–12.

Change to A.

Work 5 Rnds in dc.

Rep Rnds 6–10.

Upper Back (attached to sleeve):

ROW 1: Ch 3 (counts as dc), dc in next 18 (23, 28) dc, turn leaving rem 19 (23, 29) sts unworked.

Work 5 rows in dc.

Change to C.

Work 5 rows in dc.

Fasten off. Weave in end.

Sl st last rows of sleeves together at center back.

LOWER BACK

With RS facing, join C to first st of Upper Back near armhole.

ROW 1 (RS): Ch 3 (counts as dc), dc 44 (48, 56) evenly across to 2nd marked st, turn.

Work 5 rows in dc.

Change to B.

Work 1 row in dc. Mark first and last st of this row.

Fasten off. Weave in end.

RIGHT FRONT BODICE

With RS facing, join C to marked stitch on last row of Back Bodice.

ROW 1 (RS): Ch 3 (counts as dc), work 9 dc evenly across ends of rows of back, dc in each of previously unworked 18 (23, 26) dc across edge of sleeve, turn—28 (33, 38).

Work 3 (4, 5) rows in dc.

Change to B.

Work 2 rows in hdc.

Change to A.

Work 4 (5, 5) rows in dc.

Fasten off. Weave in end.

LEFT FRONT BODICE

With WS facing, join C to marked st of back bodice. Work as for Left Front Bodice, beg by working Row 1 as a WS row.

FINISHING

SHOULDER SEAMS: With WS tog and A, sl st ends of Bodice rows to Sleeve Rows matching sts. Fasten off. Weave in end.

Lightly block sweater.

FRONT TRIM:

ROW 1: With RS facing and B, join yarn to front bottom corner of sweater, sc evenly up front, across back neck, and down opposite front to corner, turn.

ROW 2: Ch 2 (counts as hdc), hdc in next 2 sc, * ch 2, sk next 2 sc—tie opening made, hdc in next 3 sc; rep from * across to shoulder seam, hdc evenly around neckline to opposite shoulder seam; rep from * to * on opposite front. Fasten off. Weave in end.

SLEEVE TRIM: With D, join yarn to any st of foundation ch of sleeve, ch 2 (counts as hdc), hdc in each st around; join with sl st in top of beg ch-2. Fasten off. Weave in end. Rep for second sleeve.

BOTTOM TRIM AND TIES: With D, ch 100—first tie made, sc in last hdc of front trim, sc evenly around bottom of sweater, ch 100—second tie made. Fasten off. Weave in end. Lace through tie openings at front in a crisscross pattern.

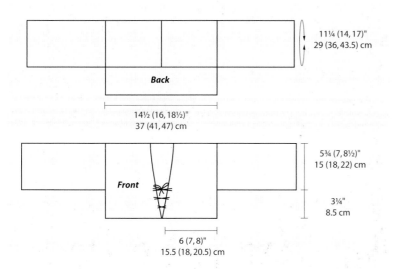

Back

11¼ (14, 17)"
29 (36, 43.5) cm

14½ (16, 18½)"
37 (41, 47) cm

Front

5¾ (7, 8½)"
15 (18, 22) cm

3¼"
8.5 cm

6 (7, 8)"
15.5 (18, 20.5) cm

gypsyduster
WITH TASSLE TIE

This breezy jacket features the illusion of a cinched waist with lacing reminiscent of a corset, while the A-line silhouette and flounced hem create fluid lines to accentuate your curves! The pattern at the cuffs and hem, along with the tassles add a vintage charm and slightly bohemian flavor. A versatile piece, this jacket can transition easily from the office to a weekend at the beach.

finished size

S (M, L), to fit 30–32 (34–36, 38–40)" (76–81 [86.5–91.5, 96.5–101.5] cm) bust circumference and 26–28 (30–32, 34–36)" (66–71.5 [76.5–81.5, 86:5–91.5] cm) waist circumference.

finished measurements

About 30 (34, 38)" (76.5 [86.5, 96.5] cm) bust circumference (exact size determined by lacing) and 34 (34½, 36)" (86.5 [88, 91.5] cm) long.

yarn

Worsted weight (#4 Medium).

WE USED: Lily Sugar n' Cream (100% cotton; 95 yd [86 m]/2 oz [56 g]): 4 (4, 5) skeins #00001 white (A), 4 (4, 5) skeins #00004 ecru (B).

hook

Size J/10 (6 mm). Adjust hook size if necessary to obtain correct gauge.

notions

Removable markers; tapestry needle.

gauge

12 dc and 6 rows = 4" (10 cm), unstretched (fabric will stretch).

DUSTER

SLEEVES

(MAKE 1 WITH A AND 1 WITH B)

Starting at bottom of sleeve and working toward shoulder, ch 36 (40, 48). Join with sl st to first ch to form circle, being careful not to twist.

RND 1: Ch 4 (counts as 1 dc and 1 ch sp), sk 1 ch, dc in next ch, ch 1, * sk 1 ch, dc in next ch, ch 1; rep from * around—36 (40, 48) sts.

RND 2: Dc in top of beg ch 3 of Rnd 1, ch 1, * dc in next ch-1 sp, ch 1; rep from * around.

RNDS 3–11: * Dc in next ch-1 sp, ch 1; rep from * around.

RND 12: Dc in next ch-1 sp, * ch 1, dc in next ch-1 sp; rep from * around, turn.

UPPER BACK

ATTACHED TO SLEEVE

ROW 1 (RS): Ch 3 (counts as 1 dc), dc in next ch-1 sp, * ch 1, dc in next ch-1 sp; rep from * 7 (8, 10) more times, turn—18 (20, 24) sts worked, leave rem 18 (20, 24) sts unworked. Mark last dc.

ROW 2: Ch 3 (counts as 1 dc), dc in next ch-1 sp, * ch 1, dc in next ch-1 sp; rep from * 6 (7, 9) more times, ch 1, sk next dc, dc in top of ch-3, turn.

ROWS 3–11 (13, 15): Rep Row 2.

Fasten off. Weave in end.

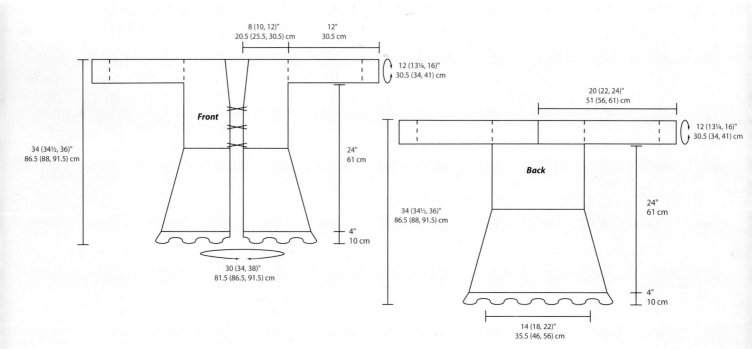

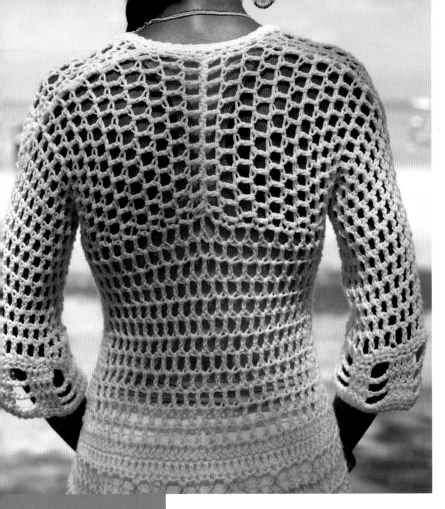

RND 6: Sc around.

Fasten off. Weave in end.

Sl st last rows of sleeves together at center back.

---

pattern note

The lower back is worked attached to the upper back between the sleeves—22 (26, 30) rows between sleeves, 11 (13, 15) rows on each side of upper back. Each row of Upper Back counts as 2 sts in Lower Back.

LOWER BACK

With RS facing, join B to first st of Upper Back near armhole.

ROW 1 (RS): Working evenly along ends of rows, ch 3 (counts as dc), dc in same row, 2 dc in next row, * ch 1, dc in next row; rep from * to last row, 2 dc in last row, turn—44 (52, 60) sts.

ROW 2: Ch 3 (counts as dc), dc in next dc, * ch 1, dc in next ch-1 sp; rep from * to last 4 dc, ch 1, sk 1 dc, dc in last 3 dc, turn.

ROW 3: Ch 3 (counts as dc), dc in next dc, * ch 1, dc in next ch-1 sp; rep from * to last ch-1 sp, dc in next ch-1 sp and last 2 dc, turn.

ROWS 4–12: Rep Rows 2 and 3 another 4 times, then rep Row 2 once more.

Fasten off. Weave in end. Mark first and last st of Row 12.

RIGHT FRONT BODICE

With RS facing, join B to marked stitch on Row 12 of Back Bodice.

ROW 1 (RS): Ch 3 (counts as dc), working evenly across ends of rows of back bodice with each row counting as 2 sts, dc in next 2 sts, * ch 1, dc in space of next row; rep from * to beg of sleeve. Do not fasten off or turn, continue to work (ch 1, dc in next sp) across sleeve to last st, dc last st, turn—42 (44, 48) sts.

CUFF

Work cuff on each sleeve using the same color as the remainder of the sleeve.

RND 1: Join yarn to any st of Rnd 1 of sleeve, ch 2, hdc around, inc 3 (sk 1, sk 2) sts evenly around—39 (39, 46) hdc.

RND 2: Dc in next 3 hdc, ch 4, * sk next 3 hdc, dc in next 4 hdc, ch 4; rep from * to last dc of rnd, dc in next hdc.

RNDS 3–4: Dc in next 3 dc, ch 4, * sk ch-4 lp, dc in next 4 dc, ch 4; rep from * to last dc of rnd, dc in next dc.

RND 5: Hdc in next 3 dc, * 3 hdc in next ch-4 lp, hdc in next 4 dc; rep from * to last dc, hdc in next dc.

ROW 2: Ch 3 (counts as dc), dc in next dc, dc in first ch-1 sp, * ch 1, dc in next ch-1 sp; rep from * across to last dc, dc in last dc, turn.

ROW 3: Ch 3 (counts as dc), dc in next 2 dc, ch 1, sk next dc, * dc in next ch-1 sp, ch 1, sk next dc; rep from * 5 more times, [dc in next ch-1 sp, dc in next dc] twice, ** dc in next ch-1 sp, ch 1, sk next dc; rep from ** to last 2 dc, dc in last 2 dc, turn.

ROW 4: Ch 3 (counts as dc), dc in next dc, dc in first ch-1 sp, * ch 1, sk next dc, dc in next ch-1 sp; rep from * 8 (9, 11) times, dc in next 5 dc, dc in next ch-1 sp, dc in next dc, dc in next ch-1 sp, ** ch 1, sk next dc, dc in next ch-1 sp; rep from ** to last dc, dc in last dc, turn.

ROW 5: Ch 3 (counts as dc), dc in next dc, dc in first ch-1 sp, * ch 1, sk next dc, dc in next ch-1 sp; rep from * 4 more times, dc in next 9 dc, dc in next ch-1 sp, ** ch 1, sk next dc, dc in next ch-1 sp; rep from ** to last dc, dc in last dc, turn.

ROW 6: Ch 3 (counts as dc), dc in next dc, dc in first ch-1 sp, * ch 1, sk next dc, dc in next ch-1 sp; rep from * 8 (9, 11) more times, dc in next 11 dc, dc in next ch-1 sp; ** ch 1, sk next dc, dc in next ch-1 sp; rep from ** to last dc, dc in last dc, turn.

ROW 7: Ch 3 (counts as dc), dc in next dc, dc in next ch-1 sp, * ch 1, sk next dc, dc in next ch-1 sp; rep from * 4 more times, sk next dc, dc in next 10 dc; ** ch 1, sk next dc, dc in next ch-1 sp; rep from ** to last dc, dc in last dc, turn.

ROW 8: Ch 3 (counts as dc), dc in next dc, dc in next ch-1 sp, * ch 1, sk next dc, dc in next ch-1 sp, ch 1, sk next dc; rep from * another 8 (9, 11) times, ch, sk next dc, dc in next 9 dc; ** ch 1, sk next dc, dc in next ch-1 sp; rep from ** to last dc, dc in last dc, turn.

ROW 9: Ch 3 (counts as dc), dc in next dc, dc in first ch-1 sp, * ch 1, sk next dc, dc in next ch-1 sp; rep from * another 4 times, ch 1, sk next dc, dc in next 7 dc; ** ch 1, sk next dc, dc in next ch-1 sp; rep from ** to last dc, dc in last dc, turn.

ROW 10: Ch 3 (counts as dc), dc in next dc, dc in first ch-1 sp, * ch 1, sk next dc, dc in next ch-1 sp; rep from * another 9 (10, 12) times, dc in next 4 dc; ** ch 1, sk next dc, dc in next ch-1 sp; rep from ** to last dc, dc in last dc, turn.

ROW 11: Ch 3 (counts as dc), dc in each dc and ch-1 sp across to end. Do not fasten off.
With WS tog, sc ends of bodice rows to end of sleeve. Fasten off. Weave in end.

LEFT FRONT BODICE

With WS facing, join A to marked st of back bodice. Work as for Right Front Bodice, beg by working Row 1 as a WS row.

SKIRT

(WORKED THE SAME FOR ALL SIZES)

With RS facing, join B to bottom corner of Bodice.

ROW 1 (RS): Ch 3 (counts as dc), work 87 dc evenly across bottom edge of bodice—88 sts.

Change to A.

ROW 2: Ch 3 (counts as dc), sk next dc, dc across, turn.

Change to B.

ROW 3 (INCREASE ROW): Ch 3 (counts as dc), sk next dc, dc in next 4 dc, * (ch 1, sk next dc, dc in next dc) twice, ch 1, sk next dc, (dc, ch 1, dc) in next dc; rep from * 12 more times, dc in last 5 dc, turn—114 sts.

ROW 4: Ch 3 (counts as dc), sk next dc, dc in next 4 dc, * ch 1, sk next dc, dc in next ch-1 sp; rep from * across to last 5 dc, ch 1, sk next dc, dc in next 4 dc, turn.

ROW 5: Ch 3 (counts as dc), sk next dc, dc in next 3 dc, dc in next ch-1 sp, * ch 1, sk next dc, dc in next dc; rep from * across to last 5 dc, dc in next 5 dc, turn.

ROW 6: Rep Row 4.

ROW 7: Rep Row 5.

ROW 8 (INCREASE ROW): Ch 3 (counts as dc), sk next dc, dc in next 4 dc, * [ch 1, sk next dc, dc in next ch-1 sp] twice, ch 1, sk next dc, (dc, ch 1,

RUFFLE

ROW 17 (RS): Ch 3 (counts as dc), dc in next 2 dc, * ch 4, sk next 3 sts, dc in next dc; rep from * across to last 3 dc, dc in last 3 dc, turn.

ROW 18: Ch 3 (counts as dc), dc in next 2 dc, * dc in next dc, ch 4; rep from * across to last 3 dc, dc in last 3 dc, turn.

ROW 19: Ch 3 (counts as dc), dc in next 2 dc, * 3 dc in next ch-4 lp, dc in next dc, ch 4, dc in next dc; rep from * across to last ch-4 lp, 3 dc in next ch-4 lp, dc in last 3 dc, turn.

ROWS 20 AND 21: Ch 3 (counts as dc), dc in next dc, *dc in next 5 dc, ch 4; rep from * across to last 8 dc, dc in last 8 dc, turn.

TRIM

Change to A. Hdc in each st across bottom of jacket, continue to hdc evenly around remainder of jacket to bottom, ch 2, work 3 hdc in each hdc along bottom of jacket, continue to hdc evenly around remainder of jacket a second time ending at bottom; join with sl st in beg hdc, turn, sc evenly around jacket working [ch 2, sk next sc, sc in next 3 sc] 3 times about 4" (10 cm) above skirt on both sides of front to make eyelets for weaving in ties. Fasten off. Weave in end.

Lightly block duster.

TIE

With A, ch 90. Fasten off. Weave in end. Lace tie through ch-2 lps of Jacket trim in crisscross pattern like shoelaces. With A, make 2 tassels, each 4" (10.5cm) long as foll: Cut a piece of cardboard 4½" (11.5 cm) long. Wrap the yarn around the cardboard 25 times or until it's as full as you like. Thread a 6" (15 cm) piece of yarn between the cardboard and the yarn loops and tie a knot. Slip the loops off the cardboard. Wrap another strand of yarn around the tassel near the top, just below the hanging loop. Thread both tails in a needle and hide them in the center of the tassel. Cut open the bottom loops and trim the ends evenly. Sew 1 tassel to each end of tie.

dc) in next ch-1 sp; rep from * 16 more times, ch 1, sk next dc, dc in next ch-1 sp, dc in next 5 dc, turn—148 sts.

ROW 9: Rep Row 5.

ROW 10: Rep Row 4.

ROW 11: Rep Row 5.

ROW 12: Rep Row 4.

ROWS 13 (INCREASE ROW)–15: Rep Rows 3–5—194 sts after Row 13.

ROW 16: Rep Row 4.

pulloverponcho

WITH NECK WARMER

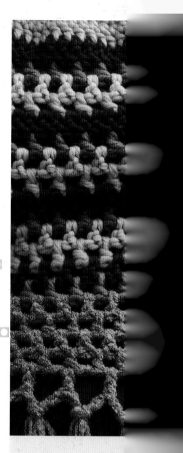

We never could figure out how to look fashionable during the cold Chicago winters . . . until now! This comfy poncho is just the right length to keep you toasty while still allowing the full range of motion you may lose underneath bulkier options. With a matching neck warmer to keep away the chill, you'll be ready to brave the cold in style.

finished size

PONCHO: S (M, L) sized to fit about 30–32 (34–36, 38–40)" (76–81 [86.5–91.5, 96.5–101.5] cm) bust circumference.

NECK WARMER: One size fits all.

finished measurements

PONCHO: 35 (39, 43)" (88.9 [99, 109.2] cm) in circumference.

NECK WARMER: 18" (46 cm) long.

yarn

Chunky weight (#5 Bulky) (A,B,C,D); Worsted weight (#4 Medium) (E).

WE USED: Rowan Big Wool (100% merino wool; 87 yd [79.5 m]/3½ oz [99 g]): Poncho—2 (2, 3) balls #025 wild berry (A); 1 (1, 2) balls #036 glamour (B); 1 (1, 2) balls #014 whoosh (C); 1 (1, 2) balls #029 pistachio (D), TLC Amoré (80% acrylic/20% nylon; 278 yd [254 m]/6 oz [170 g]): 2 (3, 3) balls #3908 raspberry (E).

hook

Size K/10½ (6.5 mm) crochet hook. Adjust hook size if necessary to obtain correct gauge.

notions

Tapestry needle; three ¾" (2 cm) buttons.

gauge

10 dc and 6 rows = 4" (10 cm).

PONCHO

With A, ch 86 (96, 106).

ROW 1: Dc in 4th ch from hook and in each ch across, turn—84 (94, 104) dc. Change to B.

ROW 2: Ch 3 (counts as dc), dc in next 3 dc, * ch 1, sk next dc, dc in next dc; rep from * across to last 4 dc, dc in last 4 dc, turn.

Change to C.

ROW 3: Ch 3 (counts as dc), dc in next 3 dc, * ch 1, sk next dc, dc in next ch-1 sp; rep from * across to last 4 dc, dc in last 4 dc, turn.

Change to D.

ROW 4: Rep Row 3.

Change to A.

ROW 5: Ch 3 (counts as dc), dc in each dc and ch-1 sp across to end, turn.

ROWS 6–12: Rep Rows 2–5 once, then rep Rows 2–4 once more.

Change to A.

ROW 13: Rep Row 3.

Change to B.

ROW 14: Rep Row 3.

Change to E.

ROWS 15–18 (20, 22): Rep Row 3.

ROW 19 (21, 23): Ch 6, dc in next dc, ch 5, sk next dc, dc in next dc, * ch 5, sk next dc and ch-1 sp, dc in next dc; ch 5, sk next ch-1 sp and dc, dc in next ch-1 sp; rep from * across to last 3 dc, dc in next dc, ch 5, sk next dc, dc in last dc. Fasten off. Weave in end.

FRINGE

Cut 180 strands, each 24" [61 cm] in length. Fold in half. Knot 6 strands held tog in each st of Row 19.

FRONT BANDS

With RS facing, Join A to beg of short edge of poncho.

ROW 1 (RS): Ch 2 (counts as hdc), working in ends of rows, hdc evenly across shorter edge.

ROWS 2 AND 3: Ch 2 (counts as hdc), hdc in each hdc across, turn.

Fasten off. Weave in end.

Rep along opposite shorter edge of poncho.

TOP BORDER

With RS facing, Join D to upper right corner of poncho.

ROW 1 (RS): Ch 3 (counts as dc), dc across top edge, turn.

ROW 2: Ch 2 (counts as hdc), hdc in each dc across, turn.

ROW 3: Change to C, rep Row 2. Fasten off. Weave in end.

FINISHING PONCHO

With B, sl st shorter edges tog from Row 1 to Row 8 to close poncho at front neckline.

Matching colors, sew ends of Top Border rows tog above center front seam.

With B, working tightly to draw in neckline, sl st in each hdc around last row of Top Border. Join with sl st. Fasten off. Weave in end.

Lightly block poncho.

NECK WARMER

With B, ch 36 (foundation ch).

ROW 1: Dc in 4th ch from hook and in each ch across, turn—34 dc.

Change to C.

ROW 2: Ch 3 (counts as dc), dc in each dc across, turn.

Change to D.

ROW 3: Rep Row 2.

Change to A.

ROWS 4–6: Rep Row 2.

Fasten off. Weave in end.

Join A to first ch of foundation ch, ch 3 (counts as dc), dc in each ch across. Fasten off. Weave in end.

Lightly block neck warmer.

BUTTONHOLE AND BUTTONBANDS

With RS facing, join A to end of first row of shorter edge.

ROW 1 (RS): Ch 3 (counts as dc), working in ends of rows, dc evenly across shorter edge of neck warmer.

ROW 2: Ch 3 (counts as dc), dc in each dc across, turn.

ROW 3 (BUTTONHOLE ROW): Ch 1, sc in next dc, * ch 2, sk next dc, sc in next 3 dc; rep from * across to last 2 dc, ch 2, sk next dc, sc in next dc.

Fasten off. Weave in end.

Repeat on other end, omitting buttonholes on Row 3 by working sc across entire row.

Sew buttons to end border to match buttonholes of opposite end border.

PAINT THE TOWN

Crochet is incredibly versatile and you can easily use it to create fabulous eveningwear. Whether you want something dramatic, romantic, or sleek and sexy, you'll find fabulous pieces that will make a statement as you paint the town. Wear an exotic feathered shrug, accentuate your curves with a feminine corset, or go glam all the way in a floor-length evening dress. You'll find lots of ideas to dress up your crochet with vivid feathers, exotic shells, or sleek satin ribbon. We hope that the unexpected details and chic styling you find here will inspire you to take your crochet to the next level to create beautiful eveningwear that is uniquely you. Once you get started, you won't want to stop!

gothicshawl
WITH TWO-WAY ZIPPER

Every woman wants to let out her inner vamp sometimes. This spiderweb-like shawl gives you the chance. Put it on over a simple dress and you have instant drama! The two-way zipper allows you to wear this piece any way you want, and the loop fringe at the neck and hem add just a touch of flair.

finished size
One size fits all.

finished measurements
88" (223.5 cm) wide when unzipped and laid flat. 24" (61 cm) circumference at neck.

yarn
Super bulky weight (#6 Bulky).

WE USED: Lion Brand Homespun (98% acrylic, 2% polyester; 185 yd [169 m]/6 oz [170 g]): 2 skeins #790-312 edwardian (A); Red Heart Light and Lofty (100% acrylic; 140 yd [128 m]/6 oz [170 g]):1 skein #9312 onyx (B).

hook
Size J/10 (6 mm). Adjust hook size if necessary to obtain correct gauge.

notions
Removable markers; tapestry needle; 29" (74 cm) black separating zipper; sewing needle and matching thread; 4 decorative beads with holes large enough to accommodate bulky yarn.

gauge
10 dc = 4" (10 cm). Row gauge is not important on this project.

SHAWL

Starting at center front and working toward hem.

With A, ch 219.

ROW 1 (RS): Hdc in 3rd ch from hook (counts as 2 hdc), hdc in each ch across, turn—218 hdc.

ROW 2: Ch 2 (counts as hdc), hdc across, turn.

ROW 3: Ch 3 (counts as dc), dc in next 3 dc, * ch 10, sk next 6 hdc, dc in next hdc; rep from * across to last 4 hdc, dc in next 4 hdc, turn—30 ch-10 lps.

ROW 4: Ch 3 (counts as dc), dc in next 3 dc, 5 dc in next ch-10 lp, * ch 10, dc in center of next ch-10 lp; rep from * across to last ch-10 lp, ch 10, 5 dc in last ch-10 lp, dc in last 4 dc, turn—29 ch-10 lps.

ROWS 5–10: Rep Rows 3 and 4 another 3 times.

Fasten off. Weave in end.

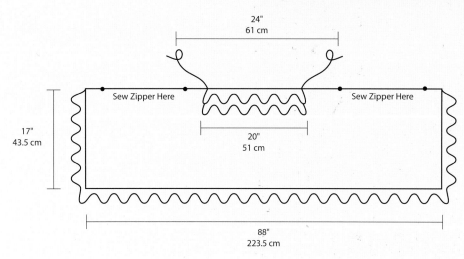

FINISHING

TRIM: Join B to first st of Row 1. Working along ends of rows, work 2 dc in each row across to corner, work 3 dc in each dc and ch across Row 9, working along opposite ends of rows, work 2 dc in each row across. Fasten off. Weave in end.

LOOP TRIM COLLAR AND TIES: Mark center 20" (51 cm) of foundation ch.

ROW 1: With A, ch 34, sc in first marked st of foundation ch, * working in blps, ch 20, sc in next sc; rep from * across to last marked st, ch 34. Fasten off. Do not turn.

ROW 2: With B, ch 34, sc in first marked st of foundation ch, * working in skipped flps, ch 20, sc in next sc; rep from * across to first marked st. Fasten off. Weave in ends. Knot beads onto ends of crochet chains.

ZIPPER: Beg about 3" (8 cm) from bottom edge, use sewing needle and thread to stitch one half of zipper to each side of center front at foundation ch, leaving center 24" (61 cm) of shawl free for neck opening.

salsabelt

WITH FRINGE

This belt was inspired by Colombian vocal artist, Shakira. We always imagine Shakira workin' this belt as she shimmies her way across the stage at a concert. Whether you're shakin' your hips at a salsa club Shakira-style or just meeting friends for a drink, the spicy color combo and long fringe will liven up your evening wardrobe. The loops along the top edge serve as buttonholes, making the belt adjustable, so wear it your way!

finished size
S (M, L) sized to fit 31–34 (36–38, 40–43)" (78.7–83.4 [91.4–96.5, 101.6–109.2] cm) hip circumference.

finished measurements
75¼ (76¾, 78)" (191.5 [195, 198.5] cm) long.

yarn
Chunky weight (# 5 Bulky).

WE USED: Schaefer Yarn, Nancy (95% merino wool, 5% nylon; 600 yd [549 m]/8 oz [100 g]): 2 (2, 3) hanks shirley chisholm (A), Caron Simply Soft (100% acrylic; 165 yd [151 m]/3 oz [85 g]):1 (1, 1) hank #2680 black (B).

hook
Size J/10 (6 mm) hook. Adjust hook size if necessary to obtain correct gauge.

notions
Tapestry needle; one 2" (5 cm) round button.

gauge
11 dc and 8 rows = 4" (10 cm) using A.

BELT

With A, ch 208 (212, 216).

ROW 1 (RS): Dc in 4th ch from hook (counts as 2 dc) and in each ch across to end, turn—206 (210, 214) sts.

ROWS 2–4 (4, 5): Ch 3 (counts as dc), dc in each dc across, turn.

RND 5 (5, 6): Ch 1, sc in each sc across, do not turn. Continue to sc evenly around, working 3 sc in each corner.

Fasten off. Weave in end.

FINISHING

EDGING: Join B to first ch of foundation ch, sc evenly across ends of rows on short end of belt, do not turn. Sc in next 3 sc, * ch 6, sk next 3 sc; rep from * across long edge of belt, sc evenly across ends of rows on short end of belt. Fasten off. Weave in end.

FRINGE: Cut 207 strands of yarn 24" (61 cm) long. Knot 3 strands of yarn held tog into first ch of foundation ch, * sk next 2 chs, knot 3 strands held tog into next ch; rep from * across remainder of foundation ch.

Sew the button to the belt about 16" (41 cm) from one end. To wear the belt, insert the button into any chain loop at the top edge of the belt to secure with a perfect fit.

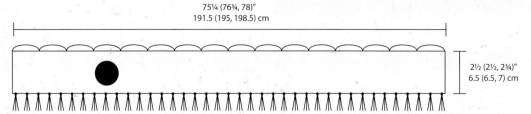

75¼ (76¾, 78)"
191.5 (195, 198.5) cm

2½ (2½, 2¾)"
6.5 (6.5, 7) cm

featherchoker

AND COCKTAIL BAG

Unique accessories can spice up any outfit, especially when you add unexpected details to the mix. This fantastic choker is embellished with feathers and cowrie shells, turning an ordinary accessory into a surefire conversation starter. The matching feathered handbag is the perfect size to carry the essentials when you are ready for a night out on the town.

finished size

COCKTAIL BAG: 5½" (14 cm) wide.

CHOKER: 7 (8¼, 9½)" (18 [21, 24.5] cm) without ties. The ties make the choker easily adjustable to desired measurements.

yarn

Worsted weight (#4 Medium).

WE USED: TLC Essentials (100% acrylic; 312 yd [285 m]/6 oz [170 g]); 1 ball #2368 dark brown (A), Patons Brilliant (69% acrylic, 19% nylon, 12% polyester; 166 yd [152 m]/1¾ oz [50 g]): 1 ball #04913 marvelous mocha (B).

hook

Size J/10 (6 mm). Adjust hook size if necessary to obtain correct gauge.

notions

Removable markers; tapestry needle; 1 package of feathers pre-sewn onto ribbon about 1 yd (.9 m) long (available at most craft stores). Sewing needle and matching thread; 5 shells with pre-drilled holes.

gauge

12 sts and 8 rows = 4" (10 cm) in hdc using A.

pattern note

The bag is worked in a continuous spiral. Do not join rounds except as indicated. You may wish to use a marker to indicate the beginning of the rnd.

COCKTAIL BAG

Ch 36. Join with sl st to form ring.

RND 1: Ch 2 (counts as hdc), hdc in each ch around — 36 hdc.

RNDS 2–9: Hdc around.

RND 10: * Sk next hdc, hdc in next 5 hdc; rep from * around — 30 hdc.

RND 11: * Sk next hdc, hdc in next 4 hdc; rep from * around — 24 hdc.
Do not fasten off.

HANDLE

Ch 36 or desired length for strap, sk next 18 hdc; join with sl st in next hdc. Fasten off. Weave in end.

BOTTOM SEAM

With WS tog, join first 18 sts to last 18 sts of Rnd 1 together with sl st across. Fasten off. Weave in end.

TRIM

With B, ch 19.

ROW 1: Ch 1, sc in each ch across, turn.

ROWS 2 AND 3: Ch 1, sc across, turn.

Fasten off. Weave in end.

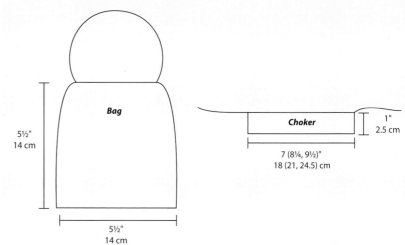

Bag

5½"
14 cm

5½"
14 cm

Choker

1"
2.5 cm

7 (8¼, 9½)"
18 (21, 24.5) cm

FEATHERS

Cut 2 strips of feathers the same length as the trim piece. Use the needle and thread to stitch 1 strip of feathers to the front of the bag about 2" (5.5 cm) from the bottom. Stitch the second piece of feathers to the WS of the trim. With RS facing, stitch the trim with attached feathers to the front of the bag about ½" (1.25 cm) from the top.

CHOKER

Ch 21 (25, 29).

ROW 1 (RS): Hdc in 3rd ch from hook (counts as 2 hdc), hdc in each ch across, turn—20 (24, 28) hdc.

ROW 2: Ch 2 (counts as hdc), hdc across. Fasten off. Weave in end.

TRIM AND TIES

Ch 24 (24, 28), sc across ends of rows on one short edge of choker, 3 sc in corner st, sc across long edge of choker, 3 sc in corner st, sc across ends of second short edge of choker, ch 24 (24, 28).

Fasten off. Weave in end.

Knot 1 shell onto the end of each tie. Sew 3 shells to front of choker in desired position.

Cut 1 piece of feather strip the same length as the center of the choker. With WS facing, stitch feathers to choker.

fittedshrug
WITH CAP SLEEVES

Want just a little something to throw on over that tank top? This teensy shrug is the perfect little something. Featuring a close fit and open-weave construction, this piece allows you the freedom to layer as you please. With this lighter alternative to a cardigan, you'll be ready to jazz up that plain top and head out for your dinner date.

finished size
XS (S, M, L) sized to fit 26–28 (30–32, 34–36, 38–40)" (66–71.5 [76–81, 86.5–91.5, 96.5–101.5] cm) bust circumference.

finished measurements
23 (27, 30, 33)" (58.5 [68.5, 76.5, 84] cm) bust circumference.

yarn
Worsted weight (#4 Medium).

WE USED: Berroco Glace 100% rayon; 75 yd [69 m]/1¾ oz [50 g]): 4 (5, 7, 8) hanks #2560 Madder Lake.

hook
Size H/8 (5 mm). Adjust hook size if necessary to obtain correct gauge.

notions
Removable markers; tapestry needle.

gauge
14 dc and 7 rows = 4" (10 cm), unstretched.

SHRUG
SLEEVES
(MAKE 2)

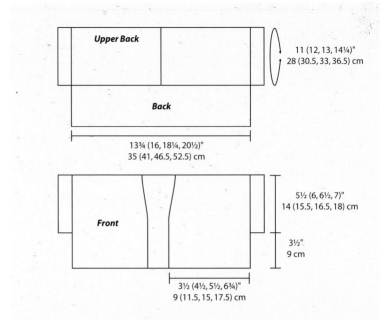

Upper Back

Back

11 (12, 13, 14¼)"
28 (30.5, 33, 36.5) cm

13¾ (16, 18¼, 20½)"
35 (41, 46.5, 52.5) cm

Front

5½ (6, 6½, 7)"
14 (15.5, 16.5, 18) cm

3½"
9 cm

3½ (4½, 5½, 6¾)"
9 (11.5, 15, 17.5) cm

pattern note

Sleeves are worked in a continuous spiral. Do not join rounds except as indicated. You may wish to use a marker to indicate the beginning of the rnd.

The lower back is worked attached to the Upper Back between the sleeves—24 (30, 34, 38) rows between sleeves, 12 (15, 17, 19) rows on each side of upper back.

Ch 38 (42, 46, 50), join with sl st in first ch to form ring.

RND 1: Ch 3 (counts as dc), dc in each ch around—38 (42, 46, 50) dc.

UPPER BACK
(ATTACHED TO SLEEVE – MAKE 2)

ROW 1 (RS): Dc in next 2 dc, * ch 1, sk next dc, dc in next 2 dc; rep from * another 5 (6, 6, 7) times, turn leaving rem dc unworked—20 (23, 23, 26) sts in row.

ROWS 2–11 (14, 16, 18): Ch 3 (counts as dc), dc in each dc and ch 1 above each ch-1 sp.

ROW 12 (15, 17, 19): Ch 3 (counts as dc), dc in each dc and ch-1 across.
Mark first and last st of last row. Fasten off. Weave in end.

Join upper back pieces by sl st last rows tog with RS facing at center back. Fasten off. Weave in end.

LOWER BACK

With RS facing, join yarn to marked st of Upper Back near armhole.

ROW 1 (RS): Working evenly along ends of rows, ch 3 (counts as dc), work 49 (55, 67, 73) dc evenly across Upper Back to second marked st, turn—50 (56, 68, 74) dc.

ROW 2: Ch 3 (counts as dc), dc in next dc, * ch 1, sk 1 dc, dc in next 2 dc; rep from * across, turn.

Rep Row 2 another 2 (3, 4, 5) times.

NEXT ROW: Ch 3 (counts as dc), dc in each dc and ch-1 sp across.

Fasten off. Weave in end.

LEFT FRONT BODICE

With RS facing, join yarn to first unworked st of Rnd 1 of First Sleeve at shoulder.

ROW 1 (RS): Ch 3 (counts as hdc), work 17 (18, 22, 23) dc evenly across unworked Sleeve sts to Lower Back, then, working across ends of Lower Back, work 8 (10, 12, 14) hdc evenly across ends of rows, turn—26 (29, 35, 38) hdc.

ROW 2: Ch 3 (counts as hdc), hdc in next hdc, * ch 1, sk next hdc, hdc in next 2 hdc; rep from * across, turn.

ROWS 3–4 (6, 8, 10): Rep Row 2.

ROW 5 (7, 9, 11): Ch 2 (counts as hdc), hdc in each hdc and ch-1 sp across, turn.

ROW 6 (8, 10, 12): Ch 2 (counts as hdc), hdc in each dc across.

Do not fasten off. With RS tog, sl st ends of Bodice rows to ends of Upper Back at shoulders. Fasten off. Weave in end.

RIGHT FRONT BODICE

Work as for Left front, beg with WS facing and working Row 1 on WS.

TRIM

ROW 1: With RS facing, join yarn to front bottom corner of shrug, sc evenly around front opening to opposite bottom corner, turn.

ROW 2: Ch 1, sc in each sc around front opening, do not turn.

RND 3: Sc evenly around entire piece working 3 sc in each corner st.

RND 4: Sc in each sc around working 3 sc in each corner st. Join with sl st in beg sc.

Fasten off. Weave in end.

Lightly block shrug.

reversehalter

SWEATER

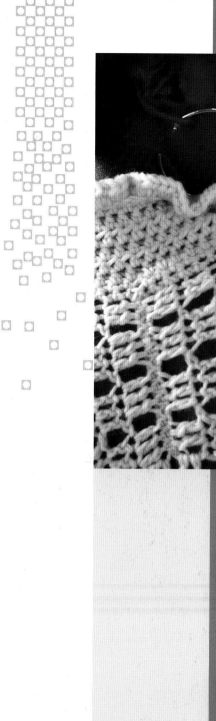

This sweater merges the demure, feminine feel of a high ruffled collar with the flirtatious quality of a plunging neckline and a cropped hem. The fluffy yarn used at the bottom is crocheted into a loose web, so you can layer to your heart's content. Wear this over a lacy camisole or alone for a distinctly romantic twist on the winter sweater.

finished size

S (M, L), sized to fit 30–32 (34–36, 38–40)" (76–81 [86.5–91.5, 96.5–101.5] cm) bust circumference and 26–28 (30–32, 34–36)" (66–71.5 [76.5–81.5, 86.5–91.5] cm) waist circumference.

finished measurements

26 (29, 32)" (66 [74, 81.5] cm) waist circumference and about 34 (38, 42)" (86.3 [96.5, 106.7] cm) bust circumference, after blocking.

yarn

Worsted weight (#4 Medium) (A); Bulky weight (#6 Super bulky) (B).

WE USED: Lion Brand Fishermen's Wool (100% Pure Virgin Wool; 465 yd [425 m]/8 oz [117 g]): 2 (2, 3) skeins #096 natural (A).
Patons Pooch (63% acrylic, 27% wool, 10% nylon; 36 yd [33 m]/2.40 oz [70 g]): 2 (2, 3) skeins #5008 fleece (B).

hook

Size J/10 (6 mm). Adjust hook size if necessary to obtain correct gauge.

notions

Removable markers; straight pins; tapestry needle; 1 yd of ¼" (.65 cm) wide satin ribbon.

gauge

12 dc and 7 rows = 4" (10 cm).

pattern notes

Sleeves and waistband are worked in a continuous spiral. Do not join rounds except as indicated. You may wish to use a marker to indicate the beginning of the rnd.

The lower back is worked attached to the upper back between the sleeves—20 (28, 36) rows between sleeves, 10 (14, 18) rows on each side of upper back. Each row of Upper Back counts as 2 sts in Lower Back.

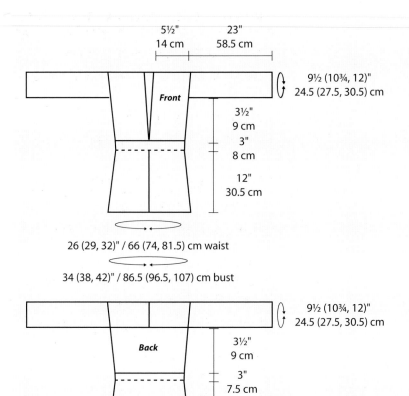

5½" 14 cm   23" 58.5 cm

Front

9½ (10¾, 12)" 24.5 (27.5, 30.5) cm

3½" 9 cm

3" 8 cm

12" 30.5 cm

26 (29, 32)" / 66 (74, 81.5) cm waist

34 (38, 42)" / 86.5 (96.5, 107) cm bust

Back

9½ (10¾, 12)" 24.5 (27.5, 30.5) cm

3½" 9 cm

3" 7.5 cm

12" 30.5 cm

SWEATER

SLEEVES

(MAKE 2)

Starting at cuff and working toward shoulder.

With A, ch 28 (32, 36). Join with sl st to form a circle.

RND 1: Ch 3 (counts as dc), dc in each ch around—28 (32, 36) dc.

RND 2: * Dc in next 3 dc, ch 1, sk next dc; rep from * around.

RNDS 3–11: Dc in each dc and ch 1 over each ch-1 sp around.

RND 12: Dc in each dc and ch-1 sp around.

RNDS 13–15 (16, 18): Dc in each dc around.

Rep Rnds 2–15 (16, 18) once, then rep Rnds 2–10 once more.

NEXT 3 RNDS: Dc in each dc and ch 1 over each ch-1 sp around to last ch-1 sp, dc in last ch-1 sp.

Do not fasten off or cut yarn.

UPPER BACK

(ATTACHED TO SLEEVE – MAKE 2)

ROW 1 (RS): Cont in patt as est, work the first 14 (16, 18) sts, turn leaving rem 14 (16, 18) sts unworked.

ROWS 2–10 (14, 18): Ch 3 (counts as dc), dc in each dc and ch 1 over each ch-1 sp across, turn.

Do not fasten off. Sl st last rows of sleeves together at center back. Fasten off. Weave in end.

LOWER BACK

With RS facing, join A to first st of Upper Back at armhole.

ROW 1 (RS): Working evenly along ends of rows, ch 3 (counts as dc), dc in next 3 sts, * ch 1, sk next st, dc in next 3 sts; rep from * across, turn—40 (56, 72).

ROW 2: Ch 3 (counts as dc), dc in next 3 dc, * dc

in next ch-1 sp, ch 1, sk next dc, dc in next 3 dc; rep from * across to last 4 dc, dc in last 4 dc, turn.

ROWS 3–6: Rep Row 2 another 4 times.

Fasten off. Weave in end. Mark first and last st of Row 6.

RIGHT FRONT BODICE

With RS facing, join A to marked stitch on Row 6 of Back Bodice.

ROW 1 (RS): Ch 3 (counts as dc) work 27 (31, 35) dc evenly across ends of rows of back and last rnd of sleeve—28 (32, 26) dc.

ROWS 2 AND 3: Ch 3 (counts as dc), dc in each dc across, turn.

ROW 4: Ch 3 (counts as dc), dc in next dc, * ch 1, sk next dc, dc in next 3 dc; rep from * across to last dc, dc in last dc, turn.

ROWS 5 AND 6: Ch 3, (counts as dc), dc in each dc and ch 1 above each ch-1 sp across, turn.

ROW 7: Ch 3 (counts as dc), dc in each dc and ch-1 sp across, turn.

ROWS 8 AND 9: Ch 3 (counts as dc), dc in each dc across.

Fasten off.

LEFT FRONT BODICE

Work as for Left front, beg with WS facing and working Row 1 on WS.

With RS tog, pin ends of Bodice rows to ends of Upper Back at shoulders, leaving center 5½" (14 cm) of back neck open. Sl st shoulder seam tog. Fasten off. Weave in end.

WAISTBAND

Join A to st at center front bottom of piece.

RND 1: Ch 1, work 80 (96, 112) sc evenly around entire bottom of piece. Join with sl st to form a circle.

RNDS 2 AND 3: Sc around.

RNDS 4 AND 5: Hdc around.

RNDS 6–8: Sc around.

RNDS 9 AND 10: Hdc around.

Do not fasten off.

PEPLUM

ROW 1 (RS): Ch 3 (counts as dc), dc in next 2 (5, 3) hdc, * ch 10, sk next 4 hdc, dc in next dc; rep from * across to last 2 (5, 3) hdc, dc in last 2 (5, 3) hdc, turn—15 (17, 21) ch-10 lps.

ROW 2: Ch 3 (counts as dc), to first ch-10 lp, 5 dc in next ch-10 lp, * ch 10, dc in center of next ch-10 lp; rep from * across to last ch-10 lp, 5 dc in last ch-10 lp, dc in last 2 (4, 5) dc, turn—14 (15, 16) ch-10 lps.

Change to B.

ROW 3: Ch 3 (counts as dc), dc in next 2 (5, 3) dc, * ch 10, dc in center of next ch-10 lp; rep from * across to last 2 (5, 3) dc, dc in next 2 (5, 3) dc, turn.

With B, rep Rows 2 and 3 another 2 times.

Fasten off. Weave in end.

FRONT AND NECK TRIM

With RS facing, join A to left shoulder at seam.

RND 1: Ch 1, sc evenly around entire front and neckline.

RND 2: Sc around, sl st in first sc to join.

Fasten off. Weave in end.

NECKBAND

Starting at bottom of band, with RS facing, join A to st that is 8 (9, 10) sts from center of back neckline.

ROW 1: Ch 1, sc in next 15 (17, 19) sts, turn.

ROWS 2–6: Ch 2 (counts as hdc), hdc across, turn.

ROW 7: Ch 2 (counts as hdc), hdc across. Do not fasten off or turn.

SIDES OF NECKBAND:

Work 7 hdc evenly across ends of Rows 2–7 of neckband, turn.

Work 5 more rows of hdc on these 7 sts.

Fasten off. Weave in end.

With RS facing, join A to end of Row 7 of neckband.

Ch 2 (counts as hdc), work 6 hdc evenly across ends of Rows 7–2 of neckband, turn.

Work 5 more rows of hdc on these 7 sts.

Do not fasten off or turn.

NECKBAND RUFFLE AND TRIM:

Working evenly across top of neckband, ch 3 (counts as dc), 3 dc in each st across, do not turn—90 (93, 96) dc.

Sc evenly around front edge to beg ch-3 of Row 1. Sl st to top of beg ch-3 to join.

Fasten off. Weave in end

To block sweater, spritz with water and stretch bodice to schematic measurements and pin to hold in place while drying.

corsettop

WITH SATIN RIBBON

This modern take on the corset will let you breath easy! You'll find no boning here, just a sleek satin ribbon to lace up the back. Wear it with jeans for a romantic touch or put it on over a simple dress for an instant wardrobe change. This project can be whipped up quickly and you can personalize it in a snap. Think about adding some fringe or crochet a decorative edging with a textured yarn.

finished size
XS (S, M, L) sized to fit 26–28 (30–32, 34–36, 38–40)" (66–71.5 [76–81, 86.5–91.5, 96.5–101.5] cm) bust circumference.

finished measurements
About 24 (28, 32, 36)" (60.9 [71.1, 81.2, 91.4] cm) bust circumference (exact circumference determined by lacing).

yarn
Bulky weight (#6 Super Bulky).

WE USED: Lion Brand Wool Ease Thick and Quick (80% acrylic, 20% wool; 106 yd [97 m]/6 oz [170 g]): 1 (1, 2) ball(s) #640-106 sky blue.

hook
Size K/10½ (6.5 mm). Adjust hook size if necessary to obtain correct gauge.

notions
Removable markers; 6 yd (5.5 m) of ⅜" (1 cm) wide satin ribbon.

gauge
8 hdc and 8½ rows = 4" (10 cm).

CORSET

Ch 49 (57, 65, 73).

ROW 1 (RS): Hdc in 3rd ch from hook (counts as hdc), hdc in each ch across, turn—48 (56, 64, 72) hdc. Mark first and last st.

ROWS 2–19 (21, 23, 25): Ch 2 (counts as hdc), hdc across.

Fasten off. Weave in end.

TRIM

With RS facing, join yarn to first marked st, working evenly in ends of rows across shorter edge, ch 2 (counts as hdc), hdc in next row, * ch 2, sk next row, hdc in next 2 rows; rep from * across to last row; working across longer edge of corset, 3 hdc in next hdc, ** hdc in next hdc, 3 hdc in next hdc **; rep from ** to ** across bottom edge of corset, continue to work in ends of rows across opposite shorter edge, hdc in next 3 sts; rep from * to * once more across to last marked st.

Fasten off. Weave in end.

Lightly block corset.

LACES

Cut ribbon into two 3 yd (2.7 m) pieces. Holding both pieces of ribbon together, start at top and weave ribbon through ch-2 sps in crisscross pattern. Tie ends in bow at bottom.

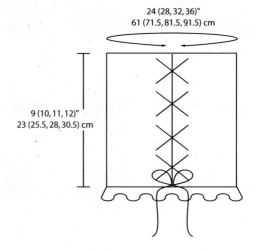

24 (28, 32, 36)"
61 (71.5, 81.5, 91.5) cm

9 (10, 11, 12)"
23 (25.5, 28, 30.5) cm

bellsleeve shrug

WITH FEATHERED COLLAR

Talk about eye candy! Show everyone just how fabulous you are when you walk into the room wearing this embellished shrug. We took a practical accessory and added a dollop of glamour with exotic, stenciled ostrich feathers. Not a fan of ostrich? No problem! You can use just about any type of feather boa (available at craft stores and online). If feathers aren't your thing, consider adding your own crocheted loop trim around the neckline (see instructions on pages 43 and 69).

finished size

S (M, L) sized to fit 30–32 (34–36, 38–40)" (76–81 [86.5–91.5, 96.5–101.5] cm) bust circumference.

finished measurements

About 5¼ (5¾, 6¼)" (13.4 [14.6, 18.9] cm) long and 56 (59½, 63)" (142.2 [151.1, 160] cm) cuff to cuff, unstretched.

yarn

Worsted weight (#4 Medium).

WE USED: Cascade Yarn Pima Silk (85% Peruvian Pima Cotton, 15% Silk; 109 yd [99.66 m]/1¾ oz [50 g]): 4 (5, 6) skeins #0010.

hook

Size G/6 (4.25 mm). Adjust hook size if necessary to obtain correct gauge.

notions

Tapestry needle; 24 (27½, 31)" (61 [69.9, 78.7] cm) length of packaged feathers, sewing needle, and matching thread.

gauge

16 dc and 7 rows = 4" (10 cm).

SHRUG

SLEEVES

(MAKE 2)

Starting at bottom of sleeve and working toward top, ch 42 (46, 50). Join with sl st to form a circle.

RND 1: Ch 3 (counts as dc), dc in each ch around—42 (46, 60) dc.

RND 2: * Dc in next dc, ch 1, sk next dc; rep from * around.

RNDS 3–6: (3–8, 3–10): *Dc in next ch-1 sp, ch 1; rep from * around.

RND 7 (9, 11): Dc in each dc and ch-1 sp around.

Rep Rnd 2 once, rep Rnd 3 another 9 times, then rep Rnd 7 (9, 11) once.

Rep Rnd 2 once, rep Rnd 3 another 4 times, then rep Rnd 7 (9, 11) once.

Rep Rnd 2 once, then rep Rnd 3 another 9 times. After completing last rnd, join with sl st in top of beg dc. Do not fasten off.

BACK
(ATTACHED TO SLEEVES)

ROW 1: Ch 3 (counts as dc), * dc in each dc and ch-1 sp until 20 (22, 29) sts have been worked— 21 (23, 30) dc.

ROWS 2–15 (17, 19): Ch 3 (counts as dc), dc in each dc across, turn.

Fasten off. Weave in end.

FRONT
(ATTACHED TO SLEEVES)

With RS facing, join yarn to first unworked st on sleeve.

Work as for back until 6 (8, 10) rows of dc have been completed. Fasten off. Weave in end.

FINISHING

Sl st last rows of back together at center back. Starting at sleeve, sew front to back at shoulder. Weave in ends.

TRIM AND TIES: Ch 45, with RS facing, join to one front corner, sc evenly across edge of front, across back, and across second front, ch 45. Fasten off. Weave in ends.

Lightly block sleeves, if desired, stretch cuffs to flare them out.

FEATHERS: Sew feathers to edge between chains at neckline.

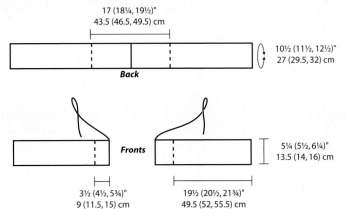

17 (18¼, 19½)"
43.5 (46.5, 49.5) cm

10½ (11½, 12½)"
27 (29.5, 32) cm

Back

Fronts

5¼ (5½, 6¼)"
13.5 (14, 16) cm

3½ (4½, 5¾)"
9 (11.5, 15) cm

19½ (20½, 21¾)"
49.5 (52, 55.5) cm

t-necktop
WITH EXTENDED SIDES

This funky little number looks like a simple halter top from the back, but the front is a whole different story! The unique T-neck design features a little added bling with some rhinestone detail along the neck. The flaps that hang down the side frame your hips, giving you the sleek silhouette of a body-hugging dress, even if you are just in jeans!

finished size
XS (S, M, L) sized to fit 26–28 (30–32, 34–36, 38–40)" (66–71.5 [76–81, 86.5–91.5, 96.5–101.5] cm) bust circumference.

finished measurements
26½ (31½, 36, 39½)" (67.5 [80, 91.5, 100.5] cm) bust circumference.

yarn
Worsted weight (# 4 Medium).

WE USED: TLC Amoré Solid (80% acrylic, 20% nylon; 278 yd [254 m]/6 oz [170 g]): 1 (1, 2, 2) skein(s) #3534 plum (A), TLC Amoré Print (80% acrylic, 20% nylon); 214 yd [195 m]/4½ oz [127 g]): 1 (1, 2, 2) skein(s) #3934 plum print (B), TLC Essentials Solid (100% acrylic; 312 yd [285 m]/6oz [170 g]): 1 (1, 1, 1) skein #2533 dark plum (C).

hook
Size J/10 (6 mm). Adjust hook size if necessary to obtain correct gauge.

notions
Removable markers; tapestry needle; 10 (11, 12, 12)" (25.5 [27.9, 30.5, 30.5] cm) separating zipper; sewing needle and matching thread; 2 pony beads; 6 rhinestones.

gauge
12 hdc and 10 rows = 4" (10 cm) using A.

HALTER

UPPER FRONT

Starting at underarms and working down, with B, ch 50 (58, 66, 74).

ROW 1 (RS): Hdc in 3rd ch from hook (counts as 2 hdc), hdc in each dc across, turn—49 (57, 65, 73) hdc.

ROWS 2 AND 3: Ch 2 (counts as hdc), hdc in each hdc across, turn.

Work even in stripe patt as foll:

ROWS 4 AND 5: With A, ch 2 (counts as hdc), hdc in each hdc across, turn.

ROWS 6–8 (6–8, 6–9, 6–9): With B, ch 2 (counts as hdc), hdc in each hdc across, turn.

ROWS 9–11 (9–12, 10–13, 10–13): With A, ch 2 (counts as hdc), hdc in each hdc across, turn.

ROWS 12–19 (13–20, 14–21, 14–21): With B, ch 2 (counts as hdc), hdc in each hdc across, turn.

ROWS 20–25 (21–27, 22–29, 22–29): With C, ch 1, sc in each st across, turn.

LOWER FRONT

Change to A.

ROW 26 (28, 30, 30): Ch 3 (counts as dc), dc in next 2 (6, 4, 4) sc, * ch 1, sk next sc, dc in next 2 sc; rep from * across to last 1 (5, 6, 5) sc, dc in last 1 (5, 6, 5) sc, turn.

ROW 27 (29, 31, 31): Ch 3 (counts as dc), dc in each dc and ch 1 above each ch-1 sp across, turn.

ROW 28 (30, 32, 32): Ch 3 (counts as dc), dc in each dc and ch-1 sp across, turn.

Do not fasten off.

RIGHT LOWER FRONT

ROW 1 (RS): Cont with A, ch 3 (counts as dc), dc in next 3 dc, * ch 1, sk next dc, dc in next dc; rep from * across 9 (11, 13, 15) times, dc in next 2 dc, turn leaving rem dc unworked—24 (28, 32, 36) sts in Right Lower Front.

ROW 2: Ch 3 (counts as dc), dc in next dc, * ch 1, dc in next ch-1 sp; rep from * across to last 4 dc, dc in last 4 dc, turn.

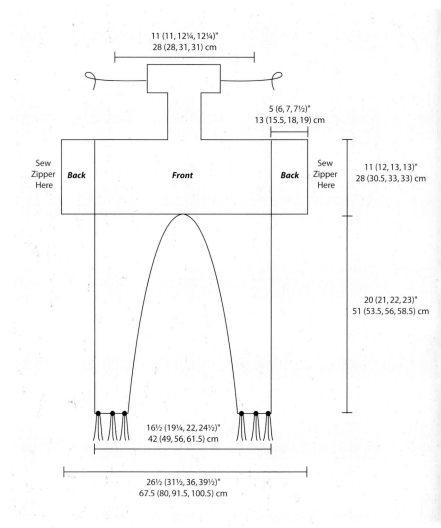

ROW 3: Ch 3 (counts as dc), dc in next 3 dc, * ch 1, dc in next ch-1 sp; rep from * across to last 2 dc, dc in last 2 dc, turn.

ROWS 4–8: Rep Rows 2 and 3 another 2 times, then rep Row 2 once more. Mark first and last sts of row 7.

Beg dec as foll:

ROW 9: Ch 3 (counts as dc), dc in next 3 dc, * ch 1, dc in next ch-1 sp; rep from * across to last ch-1 sp, dc in last ch-1 sp, turn leaving rem 2 sts unworked.

ROW 10: Ch 3 (counts as dc), dc in next ch-1 sp, * ch 1, dc in next ch-1 sp; rep from * across to last 4 dc, dc in last 4 dc, turn.

Rep Rows 9 and 10, leaving 2 sts unworked at the end of every WS row, until 16 (18, 20, 22) sts rem.

NEXT ROW (RS): Ch 3 (counts as dc), dc in next 3 dc, * ch 1, sk next dc, dc in next ch-1 sp; rep from * across to last 2 dc, dc in last 2 dc, turn.

NEXT ROW: Ch 3 (counts as dc), dc in next dc, * ch 1, sk next dc, dc in next ch-1 sp; rep from * across to last 4 dc, dc in last 4 dc, turn.

Rep last 2 rows until Right Lower Front measures about 20 (21, 22, 23)" (51 [53.5, 55, 58.5] cm).

NEXT ROW: Ch 2 (counts as hdc), hdc in each dc and ch-1 sp across.

Fasten off. Weave in end.

LEFT LOWER FRONT

With WS facing, sk 1 st at center of Upper Front and join A to next st, leaving center st unworked. Work as for Right Lower Front, except beg with Row 1 on WS.

NECK

Turn piece upside down so foundation ch is on top.

With RS facing, sk first 22 (25, 29, 33) ch, join B to next ch.

ROW 1 (RS): Ch 2 (counts as hdc), hdc in next 5 (5, 7, 7) sts, turn leaving rem ch unworked.

ROWS 2–9 (10, 10): Ch 2 (counts as hdc), hdc in next 5 (5, 7, 7) hdc, turn.

Fasten off. Weave in end.

NECKBAND

With B, ch 33 (33, 37, 37).

ROW 1: Hdc in 3rd ch from hook (counts as 2 hdc), hdc in each dc across, turn—32 (32, 36, 36) hdc.

ROWS 2–4 (2–4, 2–5, 2–5): Ch 2 (counts as hdc), hdc in each hdc across, turn. Mark first and last st of row 4 (4, 5, 5).

Fasten off. Weave in end.

Sew center 5 (5, 7, 7) sts of neckband foundation ch to top of neck. Attach rhinestones to Neckband foll manufacturer's instructions.

BACK

With RS facing, join B to marked st on Row 7 of Lower Front.

ROW 1: Working across ends of rows, ch 2 (counts as hdc), hdc evenly across to top of Upper Front, turn.

ROWS 2–6 (2–6, 2–7): Ch 2 (counts as hdc), hdc in each hdc across, turn.

Change to B.

ROW 7 (7, 8): Ch 3 (counts as dc), dc in each hdc across, turn.

ROW 8 (8, 9, 9): Ch 3 (counts as dc), dc in each dc across.

Rep Row 8 until Back measures 5 (6, 7, 7½)" (12.7 [15.3, 17.8, 19] cm) wide.

Fasten off. Weave in end.

Rep on other side, beg with WS facing.

Block halter top.

FINISHING

ZIPPER: Using needle and thread, sew half of zipper to each side of center back opening (see page 126).

TRIM: With RS facing, join C to marked st at left edge of Neckband. Ch 1, sc around edge of neckband, sc down side of neck, sc across top of Upper Front and Back to corner. Fasten off, weave in end. Rep on other side with WS facing.

NECK TIES: With C, ch 20. Fasten off. Sew tie to side edge of Neckband. Knot a pony bead onto the end of the tie. Repeat on other side.

FRONT TIES: With A, ch 65. Fasten off. Join one end of the tie just made to the skipped st between Left Lower Front and Right Lower Front. Weave in crisscross pattern like shoelaces through sts for about 5" (13 cm). Join opposite end to any st.

FRINGE: With B, knot three 24" (61 cm) strands folded in half across sts of bottom edge of Lower Fronts.

cape shawl

WITH SLEEVES

Our cape shawl combines the practicality of a cardigan with the romance of a cape. The luxurious lacy pattern of the shawl adds a classic elegance to any outfit, while the versatile wrap-around ties maintain a contemporary edge. Ready to feel like a goddess? Combine the Cape Shawl with a sexy little outfit and be prepared to turn some heads.

finished size

S (M, L) sized to fit about 30–32 (34–36, 38–40)" (76–81 [86.5–91.5, 96.5–101.5] cm) bust circumference. This garment is worn very loosely, so these sizes are only a guide. To determine the correct size, measure your arm span from wrist to wrist and refer to finished measurements below.

finished measurements

49 (51, 53)" (124.5 [129.5, 135] cm), cuff to cuff, unstretched and 23" (58.4 cm) long.

yarn

Worsted weight (#4 Medium).

WE USED: Berroco Glace (100% rayon; 75 yd [69 m]/1¾ oz [50 g]): 4 (4, 5) hanks #2657 oyster (A), Berroco Bonsai (97% bamboo, 3% nylon; 77 yd [71 m]/175 oz [50]): 8 (8, 9) hanks #4110 shiboi clay (B).

hook

Size H/8 (5 mm). Adjust hook size if necessary to obtain correct gauge.

notions

Tapestry needle.

gauge

14 dc and 7 rows = 4" (10 cm), using A, unstretched.

CAPE SHAWL
SLEEVES (FRONT)

With A, ch 174 (180, 186).

ROW 1 (RS): Dc in 4th ch from hook (counts as 2 dc), dc in next 3 chs, * ch 1, sk next ch, dc in next 5 chs; rep from * across to last 5 chs, ch 1, sk 1 ch, dc in last 4 chs, turn—172 (178, 184) sts.

ROW 2: Ch 3 (counts as dc), dc in next 3 dc, ch 1, sk next dc, *dc in next 5 dc, ch 1, sk next dc; rep from * across to last 5 dc, dc in last 5 dc, turn.

ROW 3: Ch 3 (counts as dc), dc in next 4 dc, *ch 1, sk next ch-1 sp, dc in next 5 dc; rep from * across to last ch-1 sp, ch 1, sk next ch-1 sp, dc in last 4 dc, turn.

Change to B.

ROW 4: Ch 3 (counts as dc), dc in next 3 dc, dc in next ch-1 sp, * (ch 1, sk next dc, dc in next dc) twice, ch 1, sk next dc, dc in next ch-1 sp; rep from * across to last 5 dc, dc in last 5 dc, turn.

ROW 5: Ch 3 (counts as dc), dc in next 4 dc, * ch 1, dc in next ch-1 sp; rep from * across to last 5 dc, ch 1, sk next dc, dc in last 4 dc, turn.

ROW 6: Ch 3 (counts as dc), dc in next 4 dc, * ch 1, dc in next ch-1 sp; rep from * across to last 5 dc, dc in last 5 dc, turn.

ROW 7: Rep Row 5.

Fasten off. Weave in end.

SLEEVES (BACK)

With RS facing, join B to first ch of foundation ch.

ROW 1 (RS): Ch 3 (counts as dc), dc in each ch across, turn—172 (178, 182) dc.

ROW 2: Ch 3 (counts as dc), dc in next 4 (3, 4) dc, * ch 2, sk next 2 dc, dc in next 2 dc; rep from * across to last 3 (2, 3) dc, dc in last 3 (2, 3) dc, turn.

ROW 3: Ch 3 (counts as dc), dc in next 2 (1, 2) dc, * ch 2, sk next 2 dc, 2 dc in next ch-2 sp; rep from * across to last 5 (4, 5) dc, dc in last 5 (4, 5) dc, turn.

ROW 4: Ch 3 (counts as dc), dc in next 4 (3, 4) dc, * ch 2, sk next 2 dc, 2 dc in next ch-2 sp; rep from * across to last 5 (4, 5) dc, dc in last 5 (4, 5) dc, turn.

Change to A.

ROW 5: Ch 3 (counts as dc), dc in each dc and ch-1 sp across, turn.

ROW 6: Ch 3 (counts as dc), dc in next 4 (3, 4) dc, * ch 1, sk next dc, dc in next 3 dc; rep from * across to last 2 dc, dc in last 2 dc, turn.

ROWS 7 AND 8: Ch 3 (counts as dc), dc in each dc and ch 1 over each ch-1 sp across.

Fasten off. Weave in end.

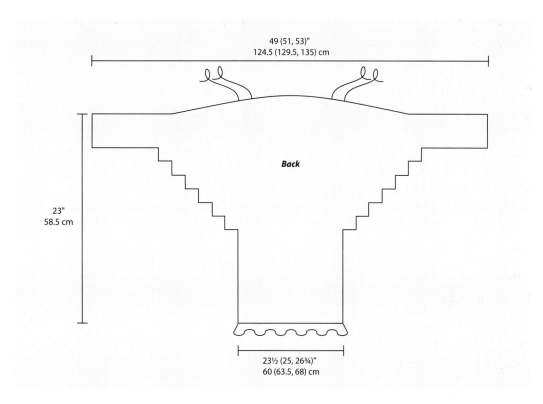

49 (51, 53)"
124.5 (129.5, 135) cm

23"
58.5 cm

Back

23½ (25, 26¾)"
60 (63.5, 68) cm

BODY

With RS facing, sk first 25 sts, join B to next st.

FIRST DECREASE:

ROW 1 (RS): Ch 3 (counts as dc), dc in next 121 (127, 133) dc and ch-1 sps, turn leaving last 25 sts unworked—122 (128, 134) dc.

ROW 2: Ch 3 (counts as dc), dc in next 3 dc, * ch 1, sk next dc, dc in next dc; rep from * across to last 4 dc, dc in last 4 dc, turn.

SECOND DECREASE:

ROW 3: Ch 1 (does not count as st), sl st in base of ch and next 3 sts, ch 3 (counts as dc), dc in next ch-1 sp, * ch 1, dc in next ch-1 sp; rep from * across to last 7 sts, dc in next 3 sts, turn leaving last 4 sts unworked.

ROW 4: Ch 3 (counts as dc), dc in next dc, * ch 1, dc in next ch-1 sp; rep from * across to last ch-1 sp, dc in last ch-1 sp and last 2 dc, turn.

THIRD DECREASE:

ROW 5: Ch 1 (does not count as st), sl st in base of ch and next 3 sts, ch 3 (counts as dc), dc in next ch-1 sp, * ch 1, dc in next ch-1 sp; rep from * across to last 7 sts, dc in next 3 sts, turn leaving last 4 sts unworked.

ROW 6: Ch 3 (counts as dc), dc in each dc and ch-1 sp across, turn.

FOURTH DECREASE:

ROW 7: Ch 1 (does not count as st), sl st in base of ch and next 3 sts, ch 3 (counts as dc), dc in next dc, * ch 1, sk next dc, dc in next 2 dc; rep

from * across to last 7 sts, dc in next 3 sts, turn leaving last 4 sts unworked.

ROW 8: Ch 3 (counts as dc), dc in each dc and ch 1 above each ch-1 sp across, turn.

FIFTH DECREASE:

ROW 9: Ch 1 (does not count as st), sl st in base of ch and next 3 sts, ch 3 (counts as dc), (dc in each dc and ch 1 above each ch-1 space) across to last 4 sts, turn leaving last 4 sts unworked.

ROW 10: Ch 3 (counts as dc), dc in each dc and ch 1 above each ch-1 sp across, turn.

SIXTH DECREASE:

ROW 11: Ch 1 (does not count as st), sl st in base of ch and next 3 sts, ch 3 (counts as dc), dc in next 2 dc, * ch 1, sk next ch-1 sp, dc in next 5 dc and ch-1 sps; rep from * across to last 9 sts, ch 1, sk next ch-1 sp, dc in next 4 dc and ch-1 sps, turn leaving last 4 sts unworked.

ROW 12: Ch 3 (counts as dc), dc in next 3 dc and next ch-1 sp, * ch 1, sk next dc, dc in next 5 dc and ch-1 sps; rep from * across to last 3 dc, dc in last 3 dc, turn.

Continue to work on 82 (88, 94) rem sts with no further shaping as foll:

ROW 13: Ch 3 (counts as dc), dc in next 6 dc, * ch 1, sk next dc, dc in next 5 dc and ch-1 sps; rep from * across to last 3 dc, dc in last 3 dc, turn.

ROW 14: Ch 3 (counts as dc), dc in next 5 dc, * ch 1, sk next dc, dc in next 5 dc and ch-1 sps; rep from * across to last 4 dc, dc in last 4 dc, turn.

ROW 15: Ch 3 (counts as dc), dc in next 5 dc, * ch 1, sk next dc, dc in next 2 dc; ch 1, sk next ch-1 sp, dc in next 2 dc, rep from * across to last 4 dc, dc in last 4 dc, turn.

ROWS 16–22: Ch 3 (counts as dc), dc in each dc and ch 1 above each ch-1 sp across, turn.

ROW 23: Ch 3 (counts as dc), dc in each dc and ch-1 sp across, turn.

Do not fasten off.

RUFFLE

ROW 1: Ch 3 (counts as dc), 2 dc in base of beg ch-3, 3 dc in each dc across.

Fasten off. Weave in end.

FINISHING

Fold sleeves in half lengthwise. Sew underarm seams from cuff to start of shaping.

TIES

Mark center 82 (88, 94) sts of top edge.

ROW 1 (RS): With A, ch 100, sc across marked 82 (88, 94) sts, ch 100, fasten off. Do not turn.

ROW 2 (RS): With B, ch 100, sk first 6 sts of Row 1, sc to last 6 sts of Row 1, ch 100, fasten off.

Weave in ends.

shrunkenjacket
WITH ATTACHED SCARF

Want to add a flourish to your outfit but don't want to wear a structured blazer? The shrunken jacket gives you the option of a little cover with the comfort and ease of crochet. The slightly cinched waist gives the jacket a fitted appearance, and the attached neck scarf adds the finishing touch to this polished sheath.

finished size
S (M, L) sized to fit 30–32 (34–36, 38–40)" (76–81 [86.5–91.5, 96.5–101.5] cm) bust circumference.

finished measurements
29 (33, 36)" (73.7 [83.9, 91.4] cm) bust circumference. This sweater is meant to be worn open and does not close in front.

yarn
Light worsted weight (#3 Light).

WE USED: Blue Sky Alpacas Alpaca Silk (50% alpaca, 50% silk; 146 yd [134 m]/ 1¾ oz [50 g]): 3 (4, 4) skeins #137 sapphire (A); 2 (3, 3) skeins #139 peacock (B).

hook
Size J/10 (6 mm). Adjust hook size if necessary to obtain correct gauge.

notions
Removable markers; tapestry needle.

gauge
14 dc and 7 rows = 4" (10 cm).

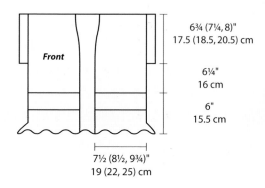

pattern note

The back bodice is worked attached to the upper back between the sleeves—26 (28, 30) rows between sleeves, 13 (14, 15) rows on each side of upper back.

JACKET

SLEEVES

(MAKE 2)

Starting at end of sleeve, with A, ch 50 (54, 58). Join with sl st to form a circle.

RND 1: Dc in 4th ch from hook and each ch across, turn—48 (52, 56) dc.

ROW 2: Ch 3 (counts as dc), dc in each dc across, turn.

UPPER BACK

(MAKE 2)

ROW 1: Ch 3 (counts as dc), dc in next 23 (25, 27) dc, turn leaving rem dc unworked—24 (26, 28) dc. Mark first and last dc.

ROWS 2–5 [2–7, 1–9]: Ch 3 (counts as dc), dc in each dc across; turn.

ROW 6 (8, 10): Ch 3 (counts as dc), dc in next 3 dc, * ch 1, sk next dc, dc in next 2 dc; rep from * across to last 4 dc, dc in last 4 dc, turn.

ROWS 7 AND 8 (9 AND 10, 11 AND 12): Ch 3 (counts as dc), dc in next 3 dc, * ch 1, sk next ch-1 sp, dc in next 2 dc; rep from * across to last 2 dc, dc in last 2 dc, turn.

ROW 9 (11, 13): Ch 3 (counts as dc), dc in each dc and ch-1 sp across, turn.

ROWS 10–13 (14, 15): Ch 3 (counts as dc), dc in each dc across, turn.

Fasten off. Sl st last rows of Upper Back together at center back. Fasten off. Sew beg and end of first 2 rows tog at underarm. Weave in ends.

LOWER BACK

With WS facing and B, join yarn to marked st of Upper Back near armhole.

ROW 1: Working evenly across ends of rows, ch 2 (counts as hdc), work 49 (55, 61) hdc evenly across to second marked st, turn—50 (56, 62) hdc.

Change To A.

ROW 2: Ch 3 (counts as dc), dc in next 2 hdc, * ch 1, sk next hdc, dc in next 2 hdc; rep from * across to last 4 hdc, dc in last 4 hdc, turn.

ROWS 3–5: Ch 3 (counts as dc), dc in next 2 dc, * ch 1, sk next dc, dc in next dc, dc in next ch-1 sp; rep from * across to last 2 dc, dc in last 2 dc, turn.

Change to B.

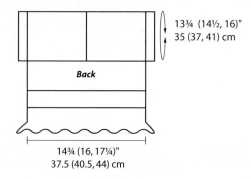

13¾ (14½, 16)"
35 (37, 41) cm

Back

14¾ (16, 17¼)"
37.5 (40.5, 44) cm

Front

6¾ (7¼, 8)"
17.5 (18.5, 20.5) cm

6¼"
16 cm

6"
15.5 cm

7½ (8½, 9¾)"
19 (22, 25) cm

ROW 6: Ch 2 (counts as hdc), hdc in each dc and ch-1 sp across, turn.

Change to A.

ROW 7: Ch 3 (counts as dc), dc in next 2 hdc, * ch 1, sk next hdc, dc in next hdc; rep from * across to last 3 hdc, dc in last 3 hdc, turn.

ROWS 8–10: Ch 3 (counts as dc), dc in next 2 dc, * ch 1, dc in next ch-1 sp; rep from * across to last 3 dc, dc in last 3 hdc.

ROW 11: Ch 2 (counts as hdc), hdc in each dc and ch-1 sp across. Mark first and last st of row.

Fasten off. Weave in end.

RIGHT FRONT BODICE

With RS facing, join A to marked stitch on last row of Lower Back.

ROW 1: Ch 3 (counts as dc), working evenly across ends of rows of back bodice with each row counting as 2 sts, work 22 dc evenly across ends of rows, work 24 (26, 28) dc across sleeve, turn—46 (48, 50) dc.

ROW 2: Ch 3 (counts as dc), dc in each dc across, turn.

ROW 3: Ch 3 (counts as dc), dc in next 2 dc, * ch 1, sk next dc, dc in next dc; rep from * across 7 [8, 9] times, dc in each rem dc across, turn.

ROW 4: Ch 3 (counts as dc), dc in each dc across to last dc before ch-1 sp, ch-1, dc in next next ch-1 sp; rep from * across to last 3 dc, dc in last 3 dc, turn.

ROW 5: Ch 3 (counts as dc), dc in base of beg ch-3, dc in next 2 dc, * ch 1, sk next dc, dc in next ch-1 sp; rep from * across 7 [8, 9] times, dc in each rem dc across, turn.

Change to B.

ROW 6: Ch 2 (counts as hdc), hdc in each dc and ch-1 sp across, turn.

Change to A.

ROWS 7–12: Rep Rows 3–5 once, then rep Rows 4 and 5 once more, then rep Row 6 once.

Change to A.

ROW 13: Ch 3 (counts as dc), dc in base of beg ch-3, dc in next 2 hdc, * ch 1, sk next hdc, dc in next hdc; rep from * across 7 [8, 9] times, dc in each rem hdc across.

Fasten off. Weave in end.

LEFT FRONT BODICE

With WS facing, join A to marked st of Lower Back. Work as for Left Front Bodice, beg by working Row 1 as a WS row..

SHOULDER SEAMS

With WS tog, sc ends of Front Bodice rows to ends of Upper Back rows.

Fasten off. Weave in end.

PEPLUM

With RS facing, join B to bottom edge of sweater.

ROW 1 (RS): Ch 2 (counts as hdc), hdc evenly across bottom of jacket, turn.

ROW 2: Ch 1, sc in each hdc across, turn.

Change to A.

ROWS 3 AND 4: Ch 1, sc in each sc across, turn.

Change to B.

ROWS 5 and 6: Rep Row 3.

Change to A.

ROWS 7–9: Rep Rows 3 and 4, then rep Row 3 once more.

ROW 10: Ch 2 (counts as hdc), hdc in each sc across, turn.

Change to A.

ROW 11: Ch 3 (counts as dc), dc in next 2 hdc, * ch 1, sk next hdc, dc in next hdc; rep from * across to last 3 hdc, dc in last 3 hdc; turn.

ROW 12: Ch 3 (counts as dc), dc in next 2 dc, *

ch 1, (dc, ch 1, dc) in next ch-1 sp; rep from * across to last 3 dc, dc in last 3 dc; turn.

ROWS 13–15: Ch 3 (counts as dc), dc in next 2 dc, * ch 1, dc in next ch-1 sp; rep from * across to last 3 dc, dc in last 2 dc; turn.

ROW 16: Ch 3 (counts as dc), dc in each dc and ch-1 sp across, turn.

Change to B.

ROW 17: Ch 1, sc in next 2 dc, * ch 4, sk next 2 dc, sc in next dc; rep from * across to last 2 dc, sc in last 2 dc. Do not fasten off or turn.

Change to A. Continue with Trim.

TRIM

ROW 1: Hdc evenly around rem sides of jacket; join with sl st in beg hdc of Row 17 of Peplum; turn.

Change to B.

ROW 2: Sc in each hdc around.

Fasten off. Weave in end.

SCARF

With B, ch 9.

ROW 1: Dc in 4th ch from hook and in each rem ch across; turn—7 dc.

ROWS 2–76 [2–78, 2–80]: Ch 3 (counts as dc), dc in each dc across, turn. Mark Row 36 [37, 38] and Row 41 [42, 43].

Do not fasten off or turn. Change to A.

Working across ends of rows, sc in next row, * ch 4, sk next 2 rows, sc in next row; rep from * across to Row 1 of scarf.

Fasten off. Weave in end.

With B, working along opposite side of scarf trim, sl st center of the scarf between markers to center back of jacket neckline.

Fasten off. Weave in end.

Lightly block jacket.

peek-a-boo

DRESS AND SHAWL

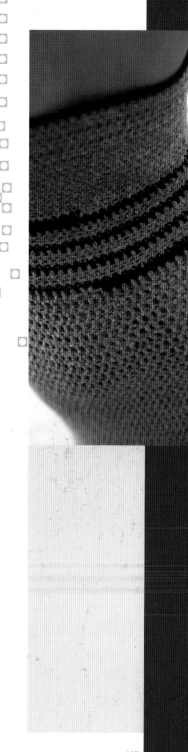

This chic update of a classic A-line knit dress gives you a fashionable alternative to the little black dress. It can be worn as a tube dress, or the straps can be tied around the neck to create a halter. A matching shawl completes the ensemble and even doubles as a scarf or a head wrap. The combination of stitches and the darker trim add visual interest, so pick your favorite color combo and go crazy!

finished size

XS (S, M, L) sized to fit 26–28 (30–32, 34–36, 38–40)" (66–71.1 [76–81, 86.5–91.5, 96.5–101.5] cm) bust circumference.

finished measurements

DRESS: 27 (31, 35, 39)" (68.5 [79, 89, 99] cm) in circumference.

SHAWL: 59 (61, 63, 65)" (150 [155, 160, 165] cm) wide by 8" [20.5 cm] long.

yarn

Worsted weight (#4 Medium) (A); Chunky weight (#5 Bulky) (B).

WE USED: TLC Amore Solid (80% acrylic, 20% nylon; 290 yd [265 m]/6 oz [170 g]): 6 (6, 6, 7) skein(s) #3908 raspberry (A); Lion Suede (100% polyester; 122 yd [110 m]/3 oz [85 g]):1 (1, 1, 2) skein(s) #210-147 eggplant (B).

hook

Size H/8 (5 mm). Adjust hook size if necessary to obtain correct gauge.

notions

Removable marker; tapestry needle.

gauge

10 sc = 4" (10 cm) using A. Row gauge is not important for this project.

pattern note

The upper portion of the dress is worked back and forth in rows to create an opening slit at the center front. The remainder of the dress is worked in a continuous spiral. Do not join rounds except as indicated. You may wish to use a marker to indicate the beginning of the round.

DRESS
BODICE

With A, ch 67 (79, 88, 97).

ROW 1 (RS): Hdc in 3rd ch from hook (counts as 2 hdc), hdc in each ch across, turn—66 (78, 87, 96) hdc.

ROWS 2–6: Ch 2 (counts as hdc), hdc across, turn.

ROW 7: Ch 2 (counts as hdc), hdc across. Do not turn.

Beg working in rnds:

RND 8: Hdc in first hdc of Row 7 to form a ring, hdc around—66 (78, 87, 96) hdc.

RNDS 9–16: Hdc around.

Work stripe patt:

RND 17: With A, hdc around.

Add B. Do not cut A.

RND 18: With B, hdc around.

Change to A. Do not cut B.

RND 19: With A, hdc around.

RNDS 20–28: Rep Rnds 17–19 another 3 times.

Cut B. Do not fasten off or cut A.

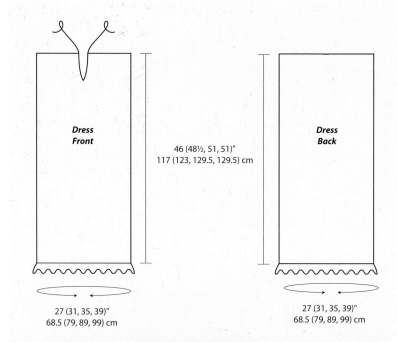

Dress Front

Dress Back

46 (48½, 51, 51)"
117 (123, 129.5, 129.5) cm

27 (31, 35, 39)"
68.5 (79, 89, 99) cm

27 (31, 35, 39)"
68.5 (79, 89, 99) cm

SKIRT

RND 1 (SIZE M ONLY): With A, dc around, inc 3 sts evenly—90 dc.

RND 1 (SIZES XS, S, AND L ONLY): With A, dc around.

RNDS 2–19 (25, 29, 29): Dc around.

RND 20 (26, 30, 30): * Ch 1, sk next dc, dc in next 5 dc; rep from * around.

RND 21 (27, 31, 31): * Dc in next ch-1 sp, dc in next 2 dc, ch 1, sk next dc, dc in next 2 dc; rep from * around.

RND 22 (28, 32, 32): * Ch 1, sk next dc, dc in next 2 dc, dc in next ch-1 sp, dc in next 2 dc; rep from * around.

Rep last 2 rnds another 9 times or until dress is 2" (5 cm) shorter than desired length. .

RUFFLE

RND 1: Dc in each dc and ch-1 sp around.

RND 2: * Ch 3, sk next 2 dc, sc in next dc; rep from * around.

RND 3: 4 dc in each ch-3 sp around.

Change to B. Cut A.

RND 4: Sc around.

Fasten off. Weave in end.

TIES

With B, ch 35 (35, 45, 45), sc in each ch of foundation ch, ch 35 (35, 45, 45).

Fasten off. Weave in end.

Lightly block dress.

SHAWL

Starting at top with A, ch 146 (152, 158, 164).

ROW 1 (RS): Dc in 4th ch from hook (counts as 2 dc), dc in each ch across, turn—144 (150, 156, 162) dc.

ROW 2: Ch 3 (counts as dc), * dc in next 5 dc, ch 1, sk next dc; rep from * across, turn.

FIRST DECREASE:

ROW 3: Sl st in next 6 sts, ch 3 (counts as dc), * dc in next 4 dc, dc in next ch-1 sp, ch 1, sk next dc; rep from * across to last 11 sts, dc in next 4 dc, dc in next ch-1 sp, turn leaving last 6 sts unworked.

ROW 4: Ch 3 (counts as dc), dc in next 3 dc, * ch 1, sk next dc, dc in next ch-1 sp, dc in next 4 dc; rep from * across to last 2 dc, dc in last 2 dc.

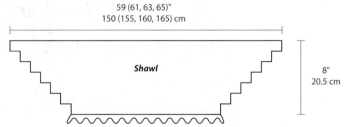

59 (61, 63, 65)"
150 (155, 160, 165) cm

Shawl

8"
20.5 cm

SECOND DECREASE:

ROW 5: Sl st in next 6 sts, ch 3 (counts as dc), dc in next ch-1 sp, * ch 1, sk next dc, dc in next 4 dc, dc in next ch-1 sp; rep from * across to last 10 sts, ch-1, sk next dc, dc in next dc, turn leaving last 6 sts unworked.

ROW 6: Ch 3 (counts as dc), dc in next dc, * ch 1, sk next dc, dc in next ch-1 sp, dc in next 4 dc; rep from * across to last ch-1 sp, dc in next ch-1 sp, dc in next 3 dc, turn.

THIRD DECREASE:

ROW 7: Sl st in next 6 sts, ch 3 (counts as dc), dc in next 3 dc, *ch 1, sk next dc, dc in next ch-1 sp; dc in next 4 dc; rep from * across to last 8 sts, dc in next 2 dc, turn leaving last 6 sts unworked.

ROW 8: Ch 3 (counts as dc), dc in next 5 dc, * ch 1, sk next dc, dc in next ch-1 sp, dc in next 4 dc; rep from * across to end of row, turn.

FOURTH DECREASE:

ROW 9: Sl st in next 6 sts, ch 3 (counts as dc), dc in next 4 dc, dc in next ch-1 sp * ch 1, sk next dc, dc in next 4 dc, dc in next ch-1 sp; rep from * across to last 11 sts, dc in next 4 dc, dc in next ch-1 sp, turn leaving last 6 sts unworked.

ROW 10: Ch 3 (counts as dc), dc in next 3 dc, * ch 1, sk next ch-1 sp, dc in next 4 dc; rep from * across to last 2 dc, dc in last 2 dc, turn.

FIFTH DECREASE:

ROW 11: Sl st in next 6 sts, ch 3 (counts as dc), dc in next dc, * ch 1, sk next dc, dc in next 4 dc, dc in next ch-1 sp; rep from * across to last 10 sts, ch 1, sk next dc, dc in next 3 dc, turn leaving last 6 sts unworked.

ROW 12: Ch 3 (counts as dc), dc in next dc, * ch 1, sk next dc, dc in next ch-1 sp, dc in next 4 dc; rep from * across to last 4 sts, dc in next 4 dc, turn.

SIXTH DECREASE:

ROW 13: Sl st in next 6 sts, ch 3 (counts as dc), dc in each dc and ch-1 sp across to last 6 sts, turn leaving last 6 sts unworked.

ROW 14: Ch 3 (counts as dc), dc in next 2 dc, ch 3, sk next 2 dc, sc in next dc; rep from * across to last 3 dc, dc in last 3 dc.

ROW 15: Ch 2 (counts as hdc), hdc in next 3 dc, * 4 hdc in next ch-3 sp; rep from * across to last 3 dc, hdc in next 3 dc. Do not turn or fasten off.

TRIM

Working along end of rows, hdc evenly along side of Shawl to top corner st. Change to B. Do not fasten off or turn. Sc in each ch across foundation ch. Change to A. Do not fasten off or turn. Working along ends of rows, hdc evenly along side of Shawl to first hdc of Row 16.

Fasten off. Weave in end.

beg	begin(s); beginning		rep	repeat; repeating
blp(s)	back loop(s)		rnd(s)	round(s)
CC	contrasting color		RS	right side
ch	chain		sc	single crochet
cm	centimeter(s)		sc2tog	single crochet 2 together
dc	double crochet		sk	skip
dc2tog	double crochet 2 together		sl st	slip(ped) stitch
est	established		sp(s)	space(s)
flp(s)	front loop(s)		st(s)	stitches
foll	follows; following		tog	together
g	gram(s)		WS	wrong side
hdc	half double crochet		yd	yard
lp(s)	loop(s)		*	repeat starting point
MC	main color		**	repeat all instructions between asterisks
mm	millimeter(s)		( )	alternate measurements and/or instructions
patt	pattern			
rem	remain(s); remaining			

Blocking

Blocking is the process used to help crocheted pieces maintain their shape and ensure that stitches are even.

To wet block, lay a towel down over an ironing board or mattress (something you can stick pins into). Spritz the entire piece with water, lay it on the towel, and pin it to the proper measurements. Allow to dry completely.

To block using steam, pin the piece down dry. Using a hot iron on the steam setting, slowly wave the iron over the entire piece, about 1" from the surface. Allow to dry completely.

Checking Gauge

To check the gauge for a project, chain about 40 stitches using the recommended hook size. Work in the stitch indicated until the piece measures at least 4" (10 cm). Lay the swatch on a flat surface and use a ruler to count the number of stitches across and number of rows down (for those patterns where row gauge is given) that are present in 4" (10 cm). Repeat in another area of the swatch to confirm. If your swatch has more stitches or rows than indicated in the pattern, use a larger hook; if it has fewer, use a smaller hook. Crochet another swatch with the new hook size to check gauge.

Crochet Chain
(CH)

Make a slipknot on hook. Yarn over hook and draw it through loop of slipknot. Repeat, drawing yarn through the last loop formed.

Slip Stitch Crochet
(SL ST)

*Insert hook into stitch, yarn over hook and draw a loop through stitch and loop on hook. Repeat from *.

Single Crochet
(SC)

Insert hook into a stitch, yarn over hook and draw a loop through stitch (Figure 1), yarn over hook and draw it through both loops on hook (Figure 2).

 fig. 1

 fig. 2

Half Double Crochet
(HDC)

*Yarn over hook, insert hook into a stitch, yarn over hook and draw a loop through stitch (3 loops on hook), yarn over hook (Figure 1) and draw it through all the loops on the hook (Figure 2). Repeat from *.

fig.1

fig.2

Double Crochet
(DC)

*Yarn over hook, insert hook into a stitch, yarn over hook and draw a loop through stitch (3 loops on hook; yarn over hook (Figure 1) and draw it through two loops, yarn over hook and draw it through the remaining two loops (Figure 2). Repeat from *.

fig.1

fig.2

Single Crochet 2 Together
(SC2TOG)

Insert hook in next stitch, yarn over hook, draw loop through stitch (2 loops on hook, Figure 1). Insert hook in next stitch, yarn over hook, draw loop through stitch (3 loops on hook). Yarn over hook and draw yarn through all 3 loops on hook (Figure 2). Completed sc2tog—1 stitch decreased (Figure 3).

Double Crochet 2 Together
(DC2TOG)

Yarn over hook, insert hook in next st, and draw up a loop (3 loops on hook), yarn over hook and draw yarn through 2 loops (Figure 1), yarn over hook, insert hook in next stitch and draw up a loop, yarn over hook, draw yarn through 2 loops (Figure 2), yarn over hook and draw yarn through the remaining 3 loops on hook (Figure 3). Completed dc2tog—1 stitch decreased (Figure 4).

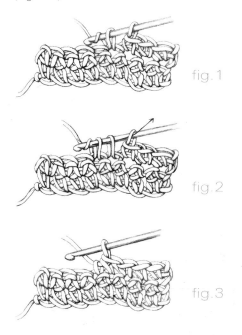

fig. 1

fig. 2

fig. 3

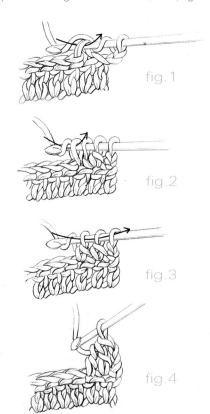

fig. 1

fig. 2

fig. 3

fig. 4

Whipstitch Seam

Hold pieces to be seamed together so that the edges to be seamed are even with each other. Thread seaming yarn on a tapestry needle and join the pieces as follows: *Insert thread needle through both layers from back to front, then bring threaded needle to back and repeat from *.

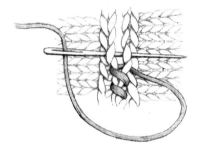

Slip-Stitch Crochet Seam

Make a slipknot with seaming yarn and place on hook. With RS of pieces facing each other, *insert hook through both pieces of fabric under the stitch loops, wrap yarn around hook to form a loop (Figure 1) and pull loop back through both pieces of fabric and through the loop already on hook (Figure 2). Repeat from *, maintaining firm, even tension.

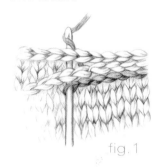

fig. 1   fig. 2

Zipper

With RS facing and zipper closed, pin zipper to fronts so front edges cover the zipper teeth. With contrasting thread and RS facing, baste zipper in place close to teeth (Figure 1). Turn work over and with matching sewing thread and needle, stitch outer edges of zipper to WS of fronts (Figure 2), being careful to follow a single column of sts in the crochet to keep zipper straight. Turn work back to RS facing and with matching sewing thread, sew crocheted fabric close to teeth (Figure 3). Remove basting.

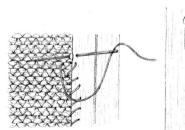

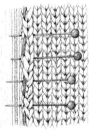

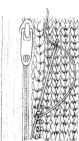

fig. 1   fig. 2   fig. 3

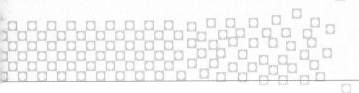

Bernat
320 Livingstone Ave. South
Listowel, ON N4W 3H3
(888) 368-8401
www.bernat.com
COOL CROCHET

Berroco Inc.
14 Elmdale Rd.
PO Box 367
Uxbridge, MA 01569
info@berroco.com
www.berroco.com
BOHO
GLACE
BONSAI

Blue Sky Alpacas Inc.
PO Box 88
Cedar, MN 55011
(888) 460-8862
sylvia@blueskyalpacas.com
www.blueskyalpacas.com
ALPACA SILK

Caron International
PO Box 222
Washington, NC 27889
public_relations@caron.com
www.caron.com
SIMPLY SOFT

Coats and Clark Inc.
PO Box 12229
Greenville, SC 29612-0229
(800) 648-1479
www.coatsandclark.com
RED HEART SOFT
RED HEART LIGHT AND LOFTY
TLC AMORÉ
TLC COTTON PLUS
TLC ESENTIALS

Cascade Yarns
www.cascadeyarns.com
PIMA SILK

Lion Brand Yarn
135 Kero Rd.
Carlstadt, NJ 07072
(800) 258-9276
FISHERMAN'S WOOL
HOMESPUN
LION SUEDE
WOOL EASE CHUNKY
WOOL EASE THICK AND QUICK

Lily
320 Livingstone Ave. South
Listowel, ON N4W 3H3
(888) 368-8401
inquire@spinriteyarns.com
www.sugarncream.com
SUGAR N' CREAM

Patons Yarns
320 Livingstone Ave. South
Listowel, ON N4W 3H3
(888) 368-8401
inquire@spinriteyarns.com
www.patonsyarns.com
BRILLIANT
POOCH

Schaefer Yarn Company Ltd.
3514 Kelley's Corners Rd.
Interlaken, NY 14847
(607) 532-9452
customerservice@schaeferyarn.com
www.schaeferyarn.com
NANCY

Westminster Fibers
5 Northern Blvd., Ste. 3
Amherst, NH 03031
www.knitrowan.com
ROWAN BIG WOOL

index

Create beautiful designs with these inspiring resources from Interweave Press

Crochet Me
Designs to Fuel the
Crochet Revolution

Kim Werker

$21.95

ISBN 978-1-59668-044-9

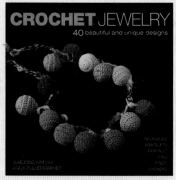

Crochet Jewelry
40 Beautiful and
Unique Designs

Waejong Kim and
Anna Pulvermakher

$24.95

ISBN 978-1-59668-035-7

**The Harmony Guides
Crochet Stitch Motifs**
250 Stitches to Crochet

Erika Knight

$22.95

ISBN 978-1-59668-083-8

**The Harmony Guides
Basic Crochet Stitches**
250 Stitches to Crochet

Erika Knight

$22.95

ISBN 978-1-59668-081-4

Interweave Crochet magazine is your single best source for crochet news, ideas, articles, and best of all—patterns!

interweavecrochet.com